The Place *of* Authority *in* Christ's Church

Jay E. Adams

TIMELESS TEXTS
Stanley, NC

Quotations from the New Testament are taken from *The Christian Counselor's New Testament,* TIMELESS TEXTS, Hackettstown, NJ, copyright © 1977, 1980, 1994 by Jay E. Adams.

© 2003 by Jay E. Adams
ISBN: 1-889032-45-X

All Rights Reserved
Printed in the United States of America

Contents

Introduction
    1. What's the Problem, Anyway?   1

Basis of Authority
    2. What is "Authority"?   5
    3. Looking at Jesus' Exousia   9
    4. Transfer of Authority   13
    5. What Does Authority Do?   17
    6. Problems with Authority   21
    7. An Authoritative Message   25
    8. The Scriptures As an Authority   31
    9. More About the Bible   35
    10. The Scriptures Have Dunamis   39

Solutions
    11. Teach with Authority   43
    12. Exhort Authoritatively   47
    13. Use Authority Fully   51
    14. Be Bold   57
    15. The Other Side of the Equation – Submission   59
    16. Limits to the Church's Authority   65
    17. Women in Authority?   69

Conclusion
    18. When All is Said and Done   79

Introduction

One sign of weakness in a church that otherwise might seem strong because of its numbers and wealth is the virtual absence of authority. Those in positions of authority tolerate heresy, and do not confront members who live as if they were pagans; worldliness in viewpoint and methodology is the order of the day, and schism is a concept outmoded among those who view as supreme the right of the individual to defect. Yes, if you didn't know, I'm talking about today's church in America at the turn of the millennium. There is something very wrong that must be addressed, dealt with, and changed, or the best of the church as we have known it for a couple of centuries past will soon disappear from the scene.

This weakness of which I speak is also clearly seen in the lack of impact that the church has upon the social, political, educational, and recreational areas of life. Millions declare their adherence to Christianity, say that they believe in the inspiration of the Bible, and hold membership in the church, but the leavening influence that they exert upon society as a whole is so minuscule that it is imperceptible. From year to year, instead, the church becomes more and more secularized as society bears a stronger and stronger influence upon it. The church is rapidly losing its distinctiveness in a politically correct culture. Pluralism reigns. And worse still, out of ignorance, fear, and whatever other causes, the church has so adapted to this culture that even many Christian publishing houses have given way to neutral gender language, the publication of heresy such as Open Theology, and the like.

What the Reformers fought so hard to achieve, what so many of their followers gave their lives to defend, is on the verge of utter disintegration. Among so-called "evangelicals," moves are afoot to cooperate with Roman Catholics, Mormons, and others in "common causes." These risky ventures, if they go unchecked, portend serious problems for Christians in the future. Many now do not know what they ought to

v

believe, others wonder about the validity of old distinctions, and some are toying with even greater union efforts based upon supposed secondary "agreements." Increasingly, tolerance for everything but true biblical intolerance is gaining the upper hand – even in some denominations that in the past have been known as staunchly biblical.

Why have these things happened? In the book, *The Use of the Rod and the Staff: A Neglected Aspect of Biblical Shepherding*, I show that the elders of the church have been shamefully negligent in pursuing their God-given duties, notably in protecting the flock from heretics, schismatics, and the like. This problem is not a uniquely modern phenomenon; it has persisted throughout the history of the church. In spite of explicit warnings from Paul, Peter, John, and other New Testament writers (not to mention Jesus, Who spoke of those who would come as "wolves in sheep's clothing"), elders have been delinquent in wielding the rod to drive away those who would devour the flock.

But there is a related issue that may explain in part why so many elders fail to stand between predators and their flocks: they do not recognize the authority that Jesus Christ has placed in their hands, or what is worse, they recognize it but fail to avail themselves of it. Surely any call to elders to wake up to the facts, to take up and use their weapons to ward off those who would intrude into Christ's flocks, and to assist in turning the current direction of things, must reemphasize the biblical warrant for such action. That warrant lies in the *authority* that Christ gave to His church.

Chapter 1
What's the Problem, Anyway?

Let's face it: people don't like authority. The mobs of protesters who follow the heads of countries around the world in order to "demonstrate" are, perhaps, the most visible evidence of this spirit of rebellion against authority in our day. They are composed of various groups: people who have failed to get their way by peaceful means such as legislation; people who would like to upset certain governments (or their leaders) because of their ideologies; and those who simply advocate anarchy. In addition, Libertarianism has been gaining popularity in this country and, to a slightly greater extreme, there are those who would completely do away with most governmental functions. It is true that government has intruded into areas that were never intended by our founding fathers to be its venues, and has assumed an all-too-pervasive and powerful place in the life of the average citizen. This intrusive nature of government has gone a long way toward providing fuel to energize those who would like to eliminate government altogether.

But coming closer to home, even in the church it is easy to detect the inroads of egalitarian thinking – most members speak and act as if Christ ordained no special office and granted no authority to exercise it. Even the officers, themselves, have so denuded their office that one would never know that Jesus expects the elders of the church to rule and teach authoritatively. Too many preachers, for instance, speak of wanting to "share" the gospel, or some other biblical truth. Share? – what a weak word! No one ever nailed anyone to the door for "sharing." Now, when one affirms, teaches, declares, proclaims, or preaches, that is a different matter. He is standing behind what he says without weakening it. But to share...? You may share an opinion, perhaps. You may offer your share of something to another, thereby indicating that you intend to offer only a part to him. But to share the gospel? Who wants only a *part* of the gospel? Preachers should present the *whole* message. Otherwise, it is no longer the gospel. When one shares a piece of pie with someone, he doesn't give him the entire pie; only a slice. And when a pastor calls on the congregation to share something along with him, he thereby levels everyone to the same non-office. His message, far from being authoritative, is viewed as only a slice of the whole which supposedly is held by the congregation. Every member's opinion carries the same weight. It places the office of teaching elder on the same plane with those who hold no office at all. In other words, any authority that the office of elder carries with it is erased by *sharing*. The office of elder has also been denuded by feminist ideology which leads to deliberate mishandling of the Scripture, thus further weakening it. When will men begin once again to preach, herald, proclaim, and declare the Word of God authoritatively instead of sharing?

Even in so-called Bible-believing churches, few recognize that the elder has been given authority to rule and manage the church. If an elder were to confront a member about persisting in sin (as he should), even in the kindest, most helpful manner, the response is likely to be "Who is he to tell me what to do? Humph!"

The democratization of the church, which Jesus did not intend to be a democracy but a theocracy in which He is the supreme Lord and King, has been running apace. It is almost to the point where, instead of a teacher preaching the authoritative Word, the congregation thinks it has the right to determine the will of God for itself. That sad departure from biblical church government has gone so far that in many congregations any elder would hardly dare to speak of exercising authority in cases that require church discipline – if, of course, he were even to think of doing so. People bristle and become stiff-necked when they are told that they are to bear the yoke and submit to the authority of Christ.[1]

---

1. The persons described in the Bible as "stiff-necked" are those who, like oxen, resist being yoked to one another and to the cart. They stiffen

What's the Problem, Anyway?

This lack of authority cries out for change. While at one time some may have misused the power Christ granted in the church, and some may have reacted against that misuse, that is no excuse for ignoring, neglecting, or defying His authority when it is rightly exercised. Nevertheless, today it is virtually missing from the church. The pendulum has swung so far to the other side that one wonders when it will ever return.

For an elder to speak to anyone in the church in an authoritative manner is almost unheard of. Yet think – if Christ has granted authority to those who hold the office of elder, they ought to exercise that authority when necessary. They are negligent if they do not do so. And consequently, the whole church suffers.

"But," says an elder, "If I speak to anyone with authority, they will think that I am pushing myself forward. They'll assume that I think I'm a holier-than-thou. I don't even dare to preach in the second person. I have to say 'we' rather than 'you.'"

"Oh? And what will Christ think if you say 'you'? Indeed, what does He think when you know you should but you don't?"

"Well..."

"Yes. Think about that. Doesn't God want you to speak authoritatively? 'We' preaching is almost on a level with 'sharing.' Consider this: God has granted authority to the church, but He has also granted authority to the state. You drive through a red light and are pulled over. The officer who stops you doesn't say, 'We went through a red light, so let's look at our licenses' as you both pull them out. 'We are going to pay a fine.'"

"No way!"

"Well, what does he say?"

"He says, '*You* went through a red light, let me see *your* license, and *you* are going to pay a fine.'"

---

their necks and make it difficult for the farmer to hitch them up. People who resist Christ's laws and the authority that He has given to the eldership are equally stiff-necked. They too make things difficult for the elders.

"You'd better believe it! He speaks with authority. And you accept his using the second person 'you,' don't you?"

"Well, yeah. But I'm not happy about the ticket I get."

"Of course you aren't, but you don't see any self-assertion in his use of the words 'you' and 'your' *per se*, do you?"

"No, I guess not. He has the authority of the state behind him, so he can speak with authority."

"Exactly. And Paul made it clear in Romans 13 that the authority of God is backed by the state's authority (see also John 19:11). And whose authority do you have backing you?"

"The authority of God?"

"You got it right in one! Why should you be hesitant when you know that God has given you authority to exert it when necessary and proper to do so?"

"Well, nobody recognizes that authority. I guess that's why."

"And how is that sad situation to be remedied? By elders copping out?"

"Well... No."

"Then one way to begin to reestablish authority in the church is to preach about it – authoritatively – and to begin to use it in the exercise of church discipline."

The truth of the matter is that many elders are simply "chicken"; they are afraid to assert the authority that Christ has given to them. They ought either to begin to do so or to resign from their office. Christ's church needs more courageous elders; there are too many wimps! Seminaries ought to teach about the authority of the eldership, and presbyteries and other ecclesiastical bodies ought to back those who practice it. It is time for the church to awaken to its responsibilities.

Chapter 2
What is "Authority"?

It is probably necessary to say just a bit about what the word "authority" means in the context in which we are using it in this book. Most people have some notion about the meaning and use of the term, but if they were called upon to define it, they would be hard pressed. We shall begin by taking a look at two Greek words that will help us to understand what is meant. The first of these is *dunamis*. This word, from which the English word "dynamite" was derived, carries the idea of power which enables one to accomplish something. There is a child's joke that goes like this: "What do you feed a 500 pound gorilla?" Answer: "Anything he wants!" That's *dunamis*! It is the power that one has, by reason of importance or might, to influence others in order to obtain what he wishes. In that sense, "authority" comes from the ethos that one's physical (or other sorts of) personal power provides. In the case of Jesus Christ, it may refer to one's personal, moral weight. It may be an authority which is valid or invalid before God. But it is, nevertheless, authority at its rawest level.

Another Greek word that is important to our discussion is *exousia*. This second term refers to one's right to do something: a right that others have conferred upon him. It is the kind of authority that the policeman in the previous chapter exerts when he stops a motorist to present him with a speeding ticket. He wears a uniform which symbolizes the fact that the power and force of the entire state backs him up in what he is doing. The state that issued him his trooper's uniform, badge, and gun did so in order to confer upon him the right to act in its behalf within the limits of his office.

When a man is elected to be an elder and hands are laid upon him, by this act the church confers the office upon him with all its responsibilities and rights. From that time forward he has been commissioned by God through His church to carry out the tasks the Bible has assigned. Heaven backs him up as he faithfully discharges those duties (Acts 18:18–20).

The individual who wears the trooper's uniform may not be the kind of person who has much personal *dunamis*. That is to say, he may not exemplify what the office stands for in his own person. He may cheat on his wife, be a very poor father, have an ungovernable temper, and the like. But unless he is found guilty of behavior unbecoming an officer of the law, he retains his conferred authority (*exousia*) and may exercise it when dealing with the public. And the public must recognize and respect his authority and obey him.

Preachers and other elders may not fit their uniform snugly either. They may fail to work diligently in the preparation of sermons, they may neglect their parishioners, and so on. But until removed from office for cause, they still retain their *exousia*. Since all are imperfect sinners, the task of the elder is to grow more and more in terms of his personal *dunamis* so that he fills out the uniform that God issued to him. In the Lord Jesus Christ we see the two in perfect correspondence with one another. In Him alone can we see what it means for *exousia* and *dunamis* to meet, each in its fullest.

As they say in the army, "Salute the uniform; not the man." This should be less true of the elder than of a soldier since God has set forth a higher standard of qualifications for the elder (see Titus 1; I Timothy 3). The goal for all elders is to become in their personal lives people whose internal *dunamis* measures up to the external *exousia* conferred upon them.

There was an authority that Jesus had with others by virtue of His presence among them. They recognized that there was something about what He did and the way in which He spoke that exhibited an *exousia* that grew out of His *dunamis*. Here is what we read:

> Now the result was that when Jesus finished these sayings, the crowds were astonished at His teaching since He taught them as an authority and not as their scribes (Matthew 7:28, 29).

The word "authority" in verse 29 is *exousia*. Literally, the phrase in the original reads, "as one having *exousia*." From

What is "Authority"?

His personal *dunamis* people concluded that He was like a person upon whom authority to teach had been conferred.[1] The assessment of Christ here is extraordinary. By the very words that He spoke (content) and the way in which he spoke them (manner), people concluded that Jesus had the right[2] to teach as He did. While He had never had men confer authority upon Him, as the scribes had, nevertheless His *dunamis*, or internal authority, was all the authority those who listened to Him needed. That *dunamis* came across to them as *exousia*. Indeed, it seems that because they so perfectly correspond to one another His listeners could not distinguish the two kinds of authority.

So, as we have been looking at these two words, we have been coming to the conclusion that "authority" is the right (*exousia*) conferred upon someone to act in some specific way or ways. We have further concluded that this person's *dunamis* ought more and more to correspond to the *exousia* by which he acts. He should wear the uniform well, filling it out in all respects. In this book, while we shall emphasize *exousia*, we shall also have occasion from time to time to speak of the need for *dunamis* among officers of the church, who represent the heavenly government. It is good to fix the import of each word in your mind before turning to the next chapter.

---

1. Of course, this was true. At His baptism Jesus received authority from God for His work.
2. *Exousia* is frequently translated "right," referring to the authority that has been conferred upon someone to do something (see also the use of *exousia* in I Corinthians 9:4–12).

Chapter 3
Looking at Jesus' *Exousia*

We saw how the crowds who heard Jesus speak responded. They attributed *exousia* (conferred authority) to Him[1] although He refused to accept the title of Rabbi, which would have meant that he had received such authority from the Sanhedrin. Yet Jesus did have authority – *divinely conferred* authority. It is that power that we will explore in this chapter.

In Luke 5, verses 17 through 26, we have the account of Jesus' healing of the paralytic. When He said to the man, "your sins are forgiven you" (v. 20), the Pharisees objected saying, "Who is this person who speaks blasphemies? Who, but God alone, can forgive sins?" (v. 21) To which objection Jesus responded as follows:

> "Why are you thinking this way in your hearts? Which is easier – to say 'Your sins are forgiven,' or to say, 'Rise and walk?' Now so that you will know that the Son of Man has authority [*exousia*] on earth to forgive sins," He said to the paralytic, "Get up and pick up your stretcher and go home." Immediately he got up before them, picked up his stretcher and went home, praising God (Luke 5:22–24).

Plainly, Jesus declared that He possessed authority to say and do what He did. Since that authority did not issue from men, it must have come directly from God. In the discussion between Jesus and the Jews found in John 5, He declared:

> Let Me assure you that the hour is coming, and now is, when the dead will hear the voice of God's Son, and those who hear will live.[2] Just as the Father has life in Himself, so too He has granted the Son to have life in

---

1. See also Mark 1:22, 27; Luke 4:32.
2. The "dead" here are those who are dead spiritually to whom Jesus granted spiritual life.

Himself. He granted Him authority [*exousia*] to pass judgment, because he is the Son of Man (John 5:25–27).

Once again, we see how Jesus asserts that He has been "granted" the right to give life to others because the Father conferred upon Him (as man) the "authority" to do so. And in His great intercessory prayer, He reiterates the fact:

> Father, the hour has come; glorify Your Son that Your Son may glorify You, since You gave Him authority [*exousia*] over all flesh so that He may give eternal life to all that You gave Him (John 17:1, 2).

There can be no doubt, then, that Jesus acted under authority duly granted to Him by the Father. That He did not act authoritatively *before* His baptism, but began to do so immediately thereafter, makes it clear that it was at that event that such authority was given to Him. The Father declared on that occasion that Jesus was His beloved Son and poured out the Spirit upon Him without measure. This event was, in effect, Jesus' installation into His mediatorial office as the Son of Man. It was the occasion on which the Father conferred upon Him all the authority of His office, only after which He went forth carrying out His mission of salvation.[1]

Finally, having carried out all that He was commissioned to do on earth, and having risen from the dead, before ascending to the mediatorial throne, Jesus said, "All authority in heaven and on earth has been given to Me" (Matthew 28:18). As the God-man, He was now about to rule over all things for the sake of His church. Paul wrote of the Father's

> mighty strength that He exerted for Christ when He raised Him from the dead, and seated Him in the heavenly places at His right hand, far above all rule and authority and power and lordship, and every name that is named not only in this age, but also in the coming

---

1. This is one reason why we can know that those spurious documents that give accounts of Jesus doing miracles as a child are entirely inconsistent with the true New Testament books.

Looking at Jesus' Exousia

one. He has subjected everything under His feet and made Him Head over all things for the sake of the church (Ephesians 1:19–22).

Here, unmistakably, Jesus is said to rule over all other powers and authorities for the benefit of His church. His authority is preeminent.

It is worthy of note that in this life and in that which follows, Jesus' ministry is *authorized* by the Father. Until the time when that authority was granted and conferred upon Him, He engaged in no official ministry. After conferral, however, all that He did He did under authority. And even now, as the God-man He is ruling and reigning supremely by the special authorization of the Father Who granted Him the right to do so.

If Jesus as the God-man could not minister except under a grant of authority, it is important to stress that those who minister today must likewise be authorized to minister. There are too many who have taken it upon themselves to minister without any authority. Speaking of the then unthinkable act of one taking upon himself the authority to minister in God's Name, the writer to the Hebrews pointed out that:

> a person doesn't take this honor upon himself, but, on the contrary, he is called by God just as Aaron was. So too, Christ didn't exalt Himself to become a High Priest, but, rather, He was appointed by the One Who said to Him, "You are My Son; I have begotten You today" (Hebrews 5:4, 5).

Throughout both Testaments we see that those ministering for God must have been duly called and authorized. Even Jesus was subject to this rule, as the writer observed. How, then, do some simply set themselves up as ministers of the church of Jesus Christ without any authorization?[1] The idea, as Hebrews 4 says, was unthinkable. Yet in our day, when

---

1. And, in some cases, even in spite of the church's *refusal* to ordain or otherwise authorize them as ministers of the new covenant.

there is so little respect for authority, no such attitude prevails. People do as they please and expect that God will be pleased as well. If I have read the Scriptures rightly, He must be greatly displeased by such willful, arrogant, anarchistic action taken in His Name.

Chapter 4
Transfer of Authority

Jesus was given *exousia* by His Father which, as we have seen, He exercised from His baptism onwards, and which He is still exercising as the God-man on the throne of heaven today. But before He ascended He gave some of that authority to His followers – especially to the disciples who would become apostles. At first, it seems that He granted authority to them for their early mission: "He appointed[1] twelve that they might be with Him and that He might send them out to preach and to exercise authority to cast out demons" (Mark 3:14, 15). But later, when He officially organized His church, it was with a grand, authoritative act that He conferred authority to forgive sins (the same authority that we saw in the previous chapter). Jesus said:

> "Peace to you. As the Father sent Me, so also do I send you." When He had said this, He breathed on them and said to them, "Receive the Holy Spirit. If you forgive anybody's sins, they are forgiven; if you retain them, they are retained" (John 20:21–23).

The missionary work that Jesus had come to do was now transferred to His apostles whom He sent in like manner as He had been sent by the Father. He commissioned them to do this work by breathing on them as a symbol that they were receiving the Holy Spirit as He had at His baptism. They were to proclaim the gospel, by which people's sins would be forgiven or retained according to whether or not they believed. This act, by which Jesus constituted His church, involved a transfer of authority. The apostles would be "sent" (as He had been) on their mission. That is, they would not speak in their own name, but would preach in the Name of the One Who sent them. It was, then, in Christ's own authority that they ministered.

---

1. Notice the authoritative language: "He appointed."

In addition, Jesus gave the great commission under His universal authority (Matthew 28:20) and instituted the authoritative process of Church discipline (Matthew 18:15 and following). This process involved "binding" and "loosing," which were authoritative acts of admitting persons into and dismissing persons from membership in His church. Unless one has been officially called as an elder and set apart for that work today, he has no right to engage in this process. But where this process does not exist, it is questionable whether we can determine that a church exists. That is true because it is church discipline that draws the line between the church and the world.

Beyond any doubt, the apostles assumed the authority which Jesus gave them. In I Timothy 6, verses 13 and 17, for instance, Paul encouraged Timothy (an elder of the church) to "instruct with authority" and "Authoritatively instruct." The word that I have translated "authoritatively instruct" (and "instruct with authority") is *paraggello*. This word was used in the papyri to describe the "official summons before a court."[1] It carried the authoritative air of an official notice or order. Paul too writes with authority to summon Timothy to keep Christ's "commandment unspotted and free from suspicion" (I Timothy 6:14). And then he urges Timothy – as one who had been officially ordained by the presbytery[2] – to "authoritatively instruct the rich" (v. 17). We can see from this passage that not only did the apostles receive authority for their work, but preaching elders in the church had received authority to pursue theirs as well. The New Testament ministers of the Word carried on their tasks under authority and with authority. There can be no question about that fact.

It is certain that the apostles passed down the authority to minister in Christ's Name to men who were appointed to

---

1. Moulton and Milligan, *The Vocabulary of the Greek New Testament*, p. 481.
2. I Timothy 4:14. In I Thessalonians 2:4–7, Paul asserts his apostolic prerogatives even when restraining from their use.

serve as elders in the church. At the Jerusalem conference (Acts 15), apostles and elders from the churches gathered to determine how to handle the Judaizing tendencies that had troubled the church. After they reached a solution, we read that "As they traveled through these cities, they delivered [to the churches] the decisions reached by the apostles and the elders at Jerusalem, and told them to *obey* them" (Acts 16:4, emphasis mine). The decisions were "reached by the apostles and the elders" jointly. They had equal authority to decide upon the matters before them. Moreover, others in the churches were to "obey" these decisions because they carried the authority to require Christians to obey.

Thus "submission" was to be given to those who served with Paul in the work of the ministry (II Corinthians 16:15, 16). And Titus was ordered by the apostle to "speak these things; urge and convict, with recognition that you have full authority to give orders. Let nobody disregard you." The Greek New Testament term translated "full authority to give orders" is *epitage*.[1] This word was used of a commander giving orders to his soldiers. Stronger still, in this very letter, the word is used of God's "order" to Paul (Titus 1:3). Moreover, Titus is instructed not to allow anyone to "disregard" the authoritative orders that he issues. The word "disregard" is a vivid one meaning, literally, "to think around." That is to say, no one was to be allowed to avoid the orders he was giving.

Similarly, the writer of Hebrews commands:

> Obey your leaders and submit to them. They are keeping watch over your lives as men who will have to give an account. Obey so that they may do this with joy and not as a burden, since that wouldn't be to your advantage (Hebrews 13:17).

There is no doubt that these elders are under authority themselves, as well as exercising authority in the church. They will have to *give an account* of their ministry among the members

---

1. The Greek reads "with all authority." That is, with complete or full authority.

of the flock. That means that they are ministering in Christ's Name (not their own) and are answerable to Him.

The authority that the apostles and the elders had was, therefore, not absolute. It was subject to the review of the Lord, Whose authority it ultimately was. Because of this, it is possible to question the authority that an elder has[1] by appealing to the written authority of the Scriptures. Elders may go wrong – and, of course, have often done so – and must be called to submit to the greater authority under which they operate.

The basic considerations that we have explored in this chapter underlie all else that I shall have to say about biblical authority, and should be kept in mind as we continue.

---

1. But not that of an inspired apostle when speaking or writing under inspiration.

Chapter 5
What Does Authority Do?

So far we have seen that all true authority is from God (cf. John 19:11). We have noted that Jesus has supreme authority in heaven and on earth as the God-man Who is seated at the right hand of God. We have further observed that He delegated part of His authority to the apostles who, in turn, granted a part of their authority to elders. So plenty of authority has been granted to the church; quite enough to bring about and keep good order. But is that the only purpose of this authority – to avoid chaos and anarchy?

In addition to an authoritative Book upon which to base one's thinking and action, there must be persons whose task is to authoritatively speak and counsel from it. These same persons should see to it that all things are done in accordance with that authoritative Book. That certainly is one major reason for the exercise of true authority: so that all things may be done decently and in order (I Corinthians 14:40).

But again let us ask, are there other reasons for giving authority to the eldership? Very definitely, yes. In II Corinthians 10:8 and 13:10, Paul tells us:

> Even if I should boast too much about the authority that the Lord gave us for building you up and not for tearing you down, I am not going to be ashamed of it... It is for this reason that I am writing these things while I'm absent, so that when I'm present I won't have to cut off any of you by the authority that the Lord gave me for building up and not for tearing down.

Clearly, Paul understood that Jesus granted him authority in order to build up the saints in their most holy faith, and to build these bodies into strong congregations that would be able withstand all that the world would throw at them. The second reason, then, is edification (or building up). Now, because he knew that in the Corinthian church there were problems standing in the way of edification, he said that he wanted to use his authority for the positive purpose of assisting them in their growth. He did not want to have to use that authority to "cut off" any from the congregation who might not give heed to these positive, edifying efforts. He wanted all to recognize and submit to the authority of Christ, in Whose Name he was writing. Yet the very mention of "cutting people off" from membership in the church clearly indicates that, if and when necessary, Paul would use his apostolic authority to do so.

How does authority build up Christians in their faith? If there were no authoritative writings such as those penned by the apostle, Christians would not be sure whether they ought to believe and do what apostles or others tell them. But as it is, not only were the apostles and prophets able to write authoritatively because the Holy Spirit spoke inerrantly through them and through their writings. In doing so, they were able to reveal the deposit of the faith once-for-all delivered to the saints, and by that authority they were also able to defend it from all errors. This was done in such a manner that those who trust in Christ might have certainty about His preceptive will. Since growth and edification are a matter of knowledge of the truth translated into life, there had to be an authoritative Source of truth. According to John 17:17, sanctification (growing more like Christ) takes place through the appropriation of God's truth. In that verse Jesus said that God's Word is "truth."

So authority helps reduce confusion and works toward order. God is a God of order Who will have all things done decently and in order. The second purpose of authority is to assure that orderly conditions prevail so as to accomplish edification. The two purposes complement one another.

There can be little or no growth under conditions of disorder. But there is a third reason that Jesus granted authority to the apostles and the elders of His church. There was more than a hint about that third purpose in the quotation from II Corinthians 13:10 when Paul spoke of not wanting to find it necessary to use his authority to "cut off" members from the church. Plainly, he knew that he had the authority to do just that. The third reason, then, is – when all persuasion fails – to eliminate any who would create confusion, disorder or intrude false teachings into the body.[1] Churches, and the individuals in them, cannot be built up when there are those in them whose sole efforts are exerted to tear them down!

This third use of authority Paul called "punishment," as, indeed, it was. He wrote:

> The punishment that the majority inflicted upon this person is sufficient; so, instead of going on with that, you should rather forgive and help him, so that he won't be overwhelmed by too much pain. Therefore, I urge you to officially reaffirm your love to him (II Corinthians 2:6–8).

Paul was writing about the repentant man whom he had previously encouraged the church to put out of their midst. Here's what he had written about this person in I Corinthians:

> Even though I am absent in body, I am present in the spirit and, as if I were present, have already made a judgment about the one who has been doing this thing. When you are assembled, and my spirit and the power of the Lord Jesus are with you, in the Name of the Lord Jesus deliver this person to Satan for the destruction of the flesh so that his spirit may be saved on the Lord's Day (I Corinthians 5:3–5).

This authoritative declaration indicates that Paul expected the church to punish this then unrepentant member by cutting him off. His words are: "Clean out the old leaven" (v. 7). Plainly, then, the third purpose of authority was, as Jesus put it, to bind and loose. So edification is the fundamental positive end in view, but when disorder occurs as the result of heresy, schism, or an unrepentant lifestyle that cannot be countenanced, a negative use of authority may be needed to reestab-

---

1. For information about protecting the flock from falsehood, see *Using the Rod and the Staff: A Neglected Aspect of Biblical Shepherding.*

lish conditions that are conducive to edification. Actually, this sort of negative action, when properly carried out, has nothing but positive effects.

It is important that those who possess authority in the church strive, as Paul did, to use that authority for purposes of edification whenever possible. There are some who like to emphasize the punishing aspects of authority; Paul sought in every way to avoid that. But he did not hesitate to resort to punishment when all else failed.[1] Does your congregation practice church discipline? Or, like the Corinthian church, does it "arrogantly" (I Corinthians 5:1–7) believe that it may deal with the problem in its own way?

---

1. There are those who think that the elder's authority is only ministerial and declarative. They do not believe that he has been granted power to legislate or to punish. Clearly, Paul thought that punishment by cutting off was a function of the eldership. And, while elders may make no laws, they have the right and obligation to legislate practical matters of good order such as when and where the congregation will meet for services.

Chapter 6
Problems with Authority

Ever since Adam fell, people have had problems with authority. There seems to be a fundamental bias against authority that manifests itself in the heart of every sinner. This bias, to put it simply, is a bias toward rebellion against God's legitimate authority. It is important to study this bias toward rebellion to see what may be done about it. There is nothing that destroys lives and congregations more than allowing this attitude to spread throughout the body. No wonder Paul referred to it as "leaven" that needed to be "cleaned out"!

Adam and Eve were the first to have a problem with authority. Since they were created good, yet capable of sinning or obeying, we do not know what it was within them that led to rebellion. The question remains, "How could a perfectly good man sin?" That is one of the few biblical questions to which Christians have no satisfactory answer. But we do know that Adam rebelled against the Word of the Lord Who told him not to eat of the tree of the knowledge of good and evil. He pitted a usurper's *assumed* "authority" against the *true* authority of his Creator! And ever since, men have been born with a nature that is biased against rightful authority.

God's command in Genesis 2:16, 17 made the choice an issue of authority. Who was the true authority? Was it God or was it Satan? Whose word was to be trusted? Whose word was authoritative? To turn from God's to Satan's word about the tree and its effects which it would have upon Adam, meant that he accepted the latter's word as authoritative. This act of rebellion was an act in which God was rejected as man's rightful Authority. Rejection of lawful authority and acceptance of unlawful authority is the very essence of rebellion.

Not only was there a rejection of God and an acceptance of the evil one; Adam's action was a bid for autonomy. *He*, rather than God, would become the final arbiter of whose word was authoritative and whose was not. *He* would be "the master of his own fate." The notion of rebellious autonomy is what has persisted in the human race, alienating man from God.

This bias for rebellion rather than for obedience seems to be so deeply embedded within the heart of man ever since Adam that it may be considered the very core sin from which all other sin flows. It is something that even believers, who have accepted God's Word about the Savior as true, still struggle with in a multitude of ways. Even after regeneration, they have difficulty accepting and following the commands of God – even though (theoretically) they know that His way is best. Sinful patterns that run deep are hard to throw off. It is not easy even for the regenerate to overcome the autonomist tendencies of the past.

This bias frequently cropped up during the entire history of Israel. Again and again we encounter a pattern of rebellion. This pattern has its most vivid expression in the stories of the golden calf and of Korah's rebellion. In these two incidents, it is interesting to examine what those in a place of authority did in dealing with the rebellion of the people. The contrast between the two occasions should be instructive to those in places of authority in Christ's church today.

When Moses went up into the mountain to receive the law, he left Aaron in charge. Because Moses did not immediately reappear, the people became impatient and determined to set up a golden calf as the god whom they would serve. This act of sheer rebellion stands as the prototype for all future rebellion against God following Adam's sin. It demonstrates that when a sinner is allowed to think that he is autonomous and fully in change of his own life, he will set up another god in place of the true One.

The exchanges between Moses and God, and then Moses and Aaron after Moses returned, are most instructive. God described the people as "stiff-necked" (Exodus 32:9). Moses asked Aaron, "What did this people do to you that you have brought this great sin upon them?" (v. 21). Aaron's answer is pitiful: he says, "You know the people yourself, that they are prone to evil" (v. 22). He then goes on to make the miserable excuse that he threw the gold into the fire and "out came this calf" (v. 24). Rebellion leads one to offer the most ridiculous reasons to justify it. Talk to elders in churches today that refuse to discipline members who clearly deserve it, and they too will offer lame excuses!

Moses saw that "the people were *let loose*" (a literal but quite expressive translation of verse 25, italics mine) because Aaron had not exerted his authority. Rather than stop them, Aaron had gone along with their rebellious request and "let them loose" (v. 25). The literal Hebrew expression "let them loose," says it all. Aaron allowed the people to have their own way, to act *autonomously* – which was to assert their own authority as final and, thereby, to rebel against the God of heaven. Because Aaron failed to exert his authority, about three thousand men were slain in one day (v. 28).

Here is a clear case of the dire consequences of the failure of a leader to use his God-given authority. Instead, he gave in to the people who, having been allowed to do as they pleased, immediately rebelled. Until elders recognize that this rebellious tendency to assert autonomy *will* manifest itself, and that if they allow people to be "let loose," the church will continue to suffer. It is their obligation, rather, to assert their authority to forestall such rebellion.

In the case of Korah's rebellion, once again we see the evil, rebellious heart of man manifesting itself. The difference was that Moses stood up against the rebellion, asserting his authority. The entire issue which arose had to do with authority. Korah charged Moses with going too far (Numbers 16:3). It was his contention that "all the people are holy," by which he meant equally capable of leading, and he leveled this further charge that Moses and Aaron had exalted themselves "above the assembly of the Lord" (v. 3). Dathan and Abiram also refused to heed Moses' authoritative summons. They too manifested the spirit of rebellion by their words:

> We will not come up. Is it not enough that you have brought us up out of a land flowing with milk and

honey to have us die in the wilderness, but would you also lord it over us? (v. 12, 13)

This time, however, Moses did not allow the people to get out of hand. Rather, he asserted his divinely given authority and took up the challenge. In response, God demonstrated that Moses had been rightly acting in His Name by opening the ground and swallowing up Korah and his entire crowd (v. 31–33). Though He will not open the ground for you to swallow up trouble-makers, elder, you can be sure that He will acknowledge your faithful use of rightly conferred authority and bless you and your church as a result.

You would think that such a denouement to Korah's rebellion would have caused the people to fear and respect the authority of Moses. But it did not. The spirit of rebellion ran so deep that "on the next day all the congregation of the sons of Israel grumbled against Moses and Aaron" (v. 41), blaming them for the deaths of those who died when the earth opened up and swallowed them. As a result, God sent a plague among the people and nearly fifteen thousand more perished (v. 46–50). It seems that people never learn! Rebellion is firmly fixed in the heart of sinful man!

In the first of these two instances, there was a failure of authority; it was an authority crisis that allowed the people to rebel. They were "let loose" so as to do what their sinful hearts dictated. This story shows clearly the importance of authority on the part of leadership among God's people. Failure to assert authority leads to rebellion which, in turn, leads to destruction. In the other instance, rebellion was checked by the assertion of rightful authority. While it did not forestall some, the rebellion of the congregation as a whole was quelled. Yet, even then, rebellion boiled over in the hearts and words of those who had just seen the hand of God at work. As a result, God purified the people by cutting off many of those who had been rejecting His authority. From these two incidents, it is possible for elders to learn the utter importance of authority rightly exercised – if only they will!

Chapter 7
An Authoritative Message

Certainly the messenger was authorized by the Lord to carry His message. In the first place, as we have seen, Jesus called His apostles the "sent off ones" (that is the meaning of the word "apostle"). An apostle is someone who has been sent off by another to do his bidding. Like an ambassador, he speaks, not for himself, but for the one who sent him. He is an *official, authoritative* representative of that person. This connection is so close that how people receive the messenger is considered equivalent to how they receive the sender. Jesus declared, "Whoever receives you receives Me, and whoever receives Me receives the One Who sent Me" (Matthew 10:40), thereby indicating that He too was an Apostle (sent off One) of the Father. It is clear, as we saw, that Jesus was the authorized Representative of the Father and that He, in turn, authorized His disciples to represent Him. Then, as He had done, they authorized the elders in the churches they planted to speak and act authoritatively in the Name of the Father, the Son and the Holy Spirit.

In order to make sure that what the elders of the various churches taught remained true (since they were not inspired men as Jesus and the apostles[1] were), the apostles gave the church a "deposit" of truth that they expected the church to "guard" so as to be able to pass it down to succeeding generations. Qualified men were to be chosen for this function so that there would be no deviation from the apostolic message. Paul wrote to Timothy,

> And the things that you heard from me before many witnesses, pass along to trustworthy persons who will be able to teach others also" (II Timothy 2:2).

---

1. For details on the inspired preaching of the apostles, see *Preaching According to the Holy Spirit*. The New Testament clearly teaches that the apostles' preaching, as well as their writing, was inerrant.

It was not enough to have authorized messengers; the message itself had to be authentic. If there was a message given in a form in which it could be retained and examined, then what preaching elders proclaimed in generations to come could be compared to the deposited message to be sure that they were preaching the truth.

That is the only way in which there could have been a Reformation. The reformers questioned the authority of the clergy of their day on the basis that neither their actions nor their message squared with the "good deposit" which the apostles bequeathed to the church. The apostles left behind that "deposit," which was the authorized apostolic message, in the form of twenty-seven inspired letters and books that we call The New Testament. This valuable deposit has been taken for granted all too often in our day. Many prefer fluffy stories to the Word of God. Today experience reigns rather than the authorized truth of a written revelation from God. And what is it that we do when we prefer someone's experience over God's Word? We set up that autonomous experience as our standard of faith and practice. It is a matter of choosing the creature over the Creator.

Giving us this deposit of His authorized truth through the inspiration of the Holy Spirit, of course, was the Lord's doing. It was not enough to ordain and authorize apostles to deposit the truth with the church. They might get it wrong. What they said and wrote had to be and remain the inspired, authentic message that they were given by God. It must not be adulterated. That is why, as Jude put it, the message was clearly known and shaped so that it could be called "the faith that was delivered to the saints in a full and final way" (Jude 3). It was in such form that it could be "delivered" to the church in one piece or package.

Paul likewise ordered Timothy to "guard that which was entrusted" to him (I Timothy 6:20). The words "that which was entrusted" are a translation of but one term in the original Greek, *paratheke*, which means "the deposit." Souter says that the word was used for "the deposit (properly of money or

An Authoritative Message

valuables deposited with a friend for safe-keeping, while the owner is abroad)."[1] What an appropriate term!

In II Timothy, Paul works out this figure of speech in some detail as he applies it to the depositing of the apostolic message. Here is what he had to say:

> Have [or hold to] the pattern of healthy words that you heard from me in the faith and love that are in Christ Jesus; guard the good deposit [*paratheke*] entrusted to you through the Holy Spirit Who dwells within us (II Timothy 1:13, 14).

Note that Paul speaks of a "pattern of healthy words" and of "the good deposit entrusted to you." Let us examine those two ideas. First, there was a deposit of that which was eminently "valuable" – more valuable than money or jewels. It was God's truth which He graciously gave to His church through authorized messengers. This truth consisted of the gospel message and all that flowed from it. Literally, the phrase "the good deposit entrusted to you" in the Greek is but two words: "my deposit." What does that mean?

Think of someone depositing money at the window of a bank. He could speak of that which he is depositing as "my deposit." That is the idea conveyed by the King James Version of verse 12 and the hymn based upon it: "that which I have entrusted unto Him against that day." But the words "my deposit," used in these verses, could be taken another way. The teller who receives the money that is deposited may also speak of that money as "my deposit." It is now *entrusted* into his hands to *guard* on behalf of the one who deposited it. And, from the context, one can readily see that it is that second thought which the apostle Paul had in mind.

When he spoke of His deposit, Paul thought of the deposit which God had given to him (v. 12) that must be "guarded" all the way up "until" the last Day. And when he spoke of passing that deposit on to Timothy, he referred to that "deposit" of truth in terms of a "pattern of healthy [sound] words" that

---

1. Alexander Souter, *A Pocket Lexicon to the Greek New Testament*.

he entrusted to him (v. 14). Because it was an exceedingly valuable deposit that he was leaving with him, he urged Timothy to "guard" it.

So it was important for the apostle to leave a "deposit" in a form (pattern) that was easily retained and passed on to "trustworthy persons" who would be "competent to teach others also." This was the method by which the authorized message was to be preserved throughout the centuries until the last Day. Paul deposited the message with Timothy (as did the other apostles chosen to write inspired material) in the form of a pattern of healthy words that he handed over to him in written form. Thus, the "good deposit" has been preserved for us in the writings of the New Testament.

All of these precautions to preserve a "deposit" and to pass on "a pattern of healthy words" indicate that the message was understood to be in a form that was depositable. It was to be preserved in that form intact. Clearly, that was what Paul had in mind when he urged Timothy to *guard* the message as something valuable. He wanted him to pass on the "authoritative" message without alteration.

If there had not been a message that was in a written form which it was possible to maintain, then it would be subject to much change through the years. And we see that when people or churches departed from the authorized form of the message as it was given in the New Testament, that is exactly what happened. As Rome departed from a scriptural base, over the years she turned more and more to extraneous accretions. This continued until, in time, it was impossible to discern the "good deposit." Untrustworthy men over the years had received the good deposit, left the original pattern in which it was found in the Bible, and distorted it beyond recognition. At the time of the Reformation, the gospel and other teachings of the apostles could not be found in the official doctrines of the Roman church. Instead, the church trusted in extraneous ideas that came from various other sources, most of which were pagan.

An Authoritative Message

But because there was a written form in which the "deposit" had been preserved, the reformers were able to scrape off the many accretions and return to the simple, saving truths that are so clearly taught in the Bible. We may thank God that "through the Holy Spirit Who dwells within us" the authorized message is still available to us today. And elders and the members of the church should not only guard that written deposit of truth, but cherish it.

So authority extends not only to the messengers who were chosen to proclaim the gospel, but also to the message which Paul was so earnestly concerned to preserve in its authoritative form. Respect for the Bible, then, ought to be uppermost in the hearts of all of God's people.

Chapter 8
The Scriptures As an Authority

There are those who debate the idea that the Scriptures are authoritative. As a cover for their unbelief, they piously claim that one can attribute authority to God alone. They call those who say that God exercises His authority over His church through authorized persons, who are committed to understanding and following the Bible, adherents to a "paper Pope." Does the Bible represent itself as the Source of authority for the life of the church in general and for the Christian's life in particular? In other words, is the Bible *the* authoritative Word from God and, if so, how does it function in such a capacity?

In addition to the concept of an authoritative, divinely-deposited Message, which we explored in part in the previous chapter, what does the Bible have to say about itself? Let's begin with the gospel – the fundamental message, which by believing, justifies a sinner before God. In I Corinthians 15:1–4, Paul set forth the two points of the good news this way:

> Now I want to remind you, brothers, of the good news that I announced to you...through which also you are saved...I delivered to you as of the greatest importance what I also received, that Christ died for our sins, in agreement with the Scriptures, and that He was buried, and that He was raised on the third day in agreement with the Scriptures.

Notice two facts. First, Paul "received" the good news from God. It was not something that he heard from men (cf. Galatians 1:1). One might say, in the words of the last chapter, that the gospel message was "deposited" with him. It was "revealed." Secondly, this gospel message Paul confirmed as from God by comparing it with the Old Testament Scriptures. As he put it, it was "in agreement with the Scriptures."[1] The Scriptures, he implied by saying so, were the authority by

---

1. That is, with the Old Testament Scriptures.

which one could determine whether or not a message was true. Clearly, Paul's double mention of scriptural agreement indicates that he was appealing to them as the final authority. If something was in agreement with the Scriptures, it was from God; it was true. This appeal to the authority of the Bible was typical of all of the Old Testament quotations found in the New Testament which were used to support what one wrote.

For instance, on one occasion Jesus cited a biblical reference as the authority for what He was teaching and then added, "the Scripture cannot be broken"[1] (John 10:34, 35). By that short, but pregnant, comment, He pointed out that the Bible is inerrant – the final authority on all issues. As the Bible was the authority for Paul, it was also for Jesus. On another occasion, He declared that those people who opposed His message were "mistaken" because they didn't know the Scriptures (Matthew 22:29).

In Luke 16:19–31, we read the account of the rich man and Lazarus. At the conclusion of the story, here is the significant observation that Abraham made:

> But Abraham said, "They have Moses and the Prophets;[2] let them hear them." But he [the rich men] said, "No, father Abraham. But if somebody from the dead goes to them, they will repent." Then he [Abraham] replied, "If they won't listen to Moses and the Prophets, they won't be persuaded even if somebody rises from the dead."

And, of course, Abraham was exactly right – many did not believe when Jesus did just that!

---

1. To be "broken" would seem to mean to be successfully challenged so as to break down what is said. That the Bible cannot be successfully challenged so as to be *refuted*, is what He had in mind. It was the final authority. Indeed, Jesus treats His quotation of Psalm 82 as if there was nothing more that needed to be said. Some would call this "proof-texting." So be it, if Jesus thought it right to do so.
2. An expression used by the Jews to refer to the entire Old Testament.

The Scriptures As an Authority

Of great significance is the import of what Abraham said. He was affirming the ultimate authority of the Bible. If it was rejected, there was nothing more to say. It was the final authority. Even the experience of a miraculous resurrection would not measure up to that. The Bible was the authority of authorities.[1] Peter, similarly, explained that written prophecy was a "more sure word" than his unique experience on the Mount of Transfiguration (II Peter 2:19). How much experience-oriented persons today could learn from Peter!

On the day of Pentecost, when the Spirit descended on the infant church, it was not to what had taken place alone that Peter appealed. Indeed, he backs up all that he says by quoting Joel 2 as the final authority for his explanation of the event: "this is what the prophet Joel spoke about" (Acts 2:16). The signs and wonders that had occurred, and would continue to occur during the last days that extended from the ministry of Christ until the destruction of Jerusalem in 70 AD, were themselves no final authority. They had to be authenticated and distinguished from other supposed miracles by God's authoritative Word.[2] Peter himself, though authorized to preach in the Name of Christ, was not the final Word. He did not think that people should accept what he said on his own word; rather, he considered it necessary to appeal to the Scriptures as the ultimate authority. And, in this regard, the Bereans' searching of the Scriptures to see whether what Paul said was true was commended by Luke (cf. Acts 17:11).

All in all, it seems apparent that in the Bible itself we have warrant for saying that the Scriptures are to be the final authority. The church may not take the place of the Bible. Churches and councils of men have erred. While what they say should be given due consideration, their declarations must be evaluated according to how well they accord with the

---

1. See also Deuteronomy 13:1–5 where a prophetic message must be compared with the known biblical understanding about God in order to test the validity of what he says. Doctrine supersedes even seemingly fulfilled signs and wonders!
2. For more on this, see my *Signs and Wonders in the Last Days*.

Scriptures. The Scriptures, then, function as what they are everywhere called "the Word of God." They are as much His holy[1] Word as if He were to speak it audibly from heaven. Contrary to those who claim that God alone has authority, and that the Scriptures do not, we may assuredly assert that between what God said verbally and what He caused to be written in the Bible, there is no difference whatsoever. God alone does have authority, but it is His prerogative to authoritatively reveal His will to His church in written form.

---

1. Unique; set apart from all other books.

Chapter 9
More About the Bible

We have seen that the Scriptures are authoritative. But what does that mean to the church and those who minister in it? Simply put – an authoritative Bible is necessary for ministry. It is no good for apostles or elders to have authority if there is no authoritative standard by which to judge their teaching and action. Apart from a divinely-given standard, they might be asserting their autonomous thoughts and ideas. And, that is precisely what has happened where the Bible has been eliminated as the authoritative Word from God.

Such a standard must both set forth the duties of each authority figure and define the limits of his authority. Otherwise the man himself becomes the standard. That is the problem, for instance, with legalists. The best known legalists are the Pharisees, who lived in Palestine in New Testament times. In order to keep people from violating the commandments of God, they built a fence of their own commandments around the law. This evolved into what Jesus called the "tradition of the elders." This tradition had so covered up the Scriptures that they were virtually smothered by it. Jesus accused the Pharisees of annulling "God's Word for the sake of [their] tradition" (Matthew 15:6).

In that statement, Jesus put His finger on the pulse of the issue. Whenever anything is added to the authoritative, sufficient written Word of God, it eventually takes precedence over the Word. That is just as true of the legalists in our day who compose lists of dos and don'ts that are not found in Scripture. Sooner or later (usually sooner) these additions shape how the legalists read the Bible. Indeed, these items on the legalist's list are for all intents and purposes his Scripture. They certainly do become the authoritative standard for his faith and life – the very thing that the Bible was intended to be. There are Pharisees in our day as well as in the time of Christ.

The answer to all legalism is found in Paul's insightful statement: "that you may learn from us not to go beyond what is written" (I Corinthians 4:6).[1] How important it is to reiterate that truth over and over again in all sorts of contexts. As Paul said, this is something that many (not only the Corinthians) need to learn.[2] People seem not to learn this on their own, so it is necessary for those who are concerned about the blight of legalism today to teach about the prohibition to "go beyond what is written." That is, they must not go beyond the good deposit of the faith. Moreover, wherever legalism persists, it should be confronted and put down. Otherwise, as we saw in the case of the Pharisees, the ideas of men will quickly take over and become the final authority, rather than the Bible.

The heart of the issue is this: is the Bible a *sufficient* authority for faith and practice or not? The question in evangelical circles today is not so much the inspiration of the Bible, but its sufficiency. Those who wish to supplement it by psychology, by marketing strategies and the like, reveal their faulty view of the divine Authority that God has so graciously given His church. Jesus said, "But when the Spirit of truth comes, He will guide you into all truth" (John 16:13). And He also put it this way: "The Holy Spirit that the Father will send in My name, He is the One Who will teach you everything and remind you of everything that I told you" (John 14:26). These two statements clearly say that the Spirit would give the apostles *everything* they needed to carry on their work. Did the Spirit do this or not? And the second statement indicates that what Jesus was referring to was *how* the Spirit would inspire them to write the New Testament books. How is that so? When He spoke of reminding them of

---

1. See also II John 8, 9. For a discussion of the II John passage see my book *The Use of the Rod and the Staff: A Neglected Aspect of Biblical Shepherding.*
2. The word for "learn" is *manthano*, which usually means "to learn by inquiry." But not every Christian inquires about the important issues. That is why they need instruction.

"everything that He told them," doubtless He was thinking of the need for supernaturally guided memories in order to write the Gospels. To write accurately they needed to be able to remember all that Jesus did and said. Peter also spoke about sufficiency when he wrote that "His divine power has given us everything for life and godliness" (II Peter 1:3). So the issue is drawn – either the Scriptures are sufficient or they are not.[1] Where do you stand on this matter?

There can be only one authoritative standard of faith and practice. The biblical Christian chooses the Bible as His one and only final standard; the legalist chooses the Bible and something else (which, as we have noted, in time will take the place of the Scriptures). That is the large issue that many need to face today. Have you dealt with this question?

---

1. See also my thorough discussion of II Timothy 3:17 in *How to Help People Change.*

Chapter 10
The Scriptures Have *Dunamis*

In the beginning of this book, I distinguished between *exousia* and *dunamis*. Because I have been speaking largely about *exousia*, and not of *dunamis*, it might be good to review briefly what the distinction between the two is. You will recall that the former is *conferred* authority, a right granted to one person by another. Jesus (as the God-man), the apostles, and the duly ordained elders of the church all possess *exousia*.[1] On the other hand, *dunamis* is what the 500-pound gorilla has; internal power to influence others. While one may have been granted *exousia*, the same person may possess only a limited amount of *dunamis*. Jesus had, to the full, both external and internal authority, each in perfect harmony with the other.

It is interesting to note that the Bible itself is said to have *dunamis*. Let's begin by looking briefly at several verses. First, Hebrews 4:12–13:

> God's Word is alive and active, sharper than any two-edged sword, penetrating deeply enough to cut open soul and spirit and joints and marrow[2]; it can judge the desires and thoughts of the heart. Before Him no creature can hide, but all are naked and laid open to the eyes of Him to Whom we must give an account.

That is *dunamis*! Scripture actively works in the lives of those whom God changes.

Clearly, the writer of the book of Hebrews taught that the Bible – which is the written Word of God – has the power to reach into the hearts of men. He speaks of it as being "active" and as "alive." It exposes and convicts people of their sin. Peter taught that it was by God's Word that the "heavens

---

1. Which ultimately was conferred by God the Father.
2. Not divide between, as some think. Rather, the sword slices each open (literally, "divides *of*") to expose what lies within.

existed and an earth was formed out of water" (II Peter 3:5). God *spoke* and there was light! Moreover, the Word is capable of "building up" believers (Acts 20:12). And that same Word is "at work" in those who "believe" (I Thessalonians 13). All of these verses clearly demonstrate the *dunamis* that God's Word possesses.[1]

The Word's *dunamis*, however, does not transform people automatically. It is hidden to the eyes and the ears of the "natural man" who looks upon it as "foolishness" (I Corinthians 2:9). And even in the case of those who *have* believed, but since that time have drifted from Scripture, it is necessary for them to resume their interest in the Scriptures and to continue studying and applying them in order to become "experienced" in discernment and grow spiritually. Otherwise, one becomes "dull" and loses his grasp even on the knowledge that he once possessed and reverts to spiritual infancy (Hebrews 5:12–14). To be positively affected by God's Word, then, one must be regenerate, come to it in faith,[2] and then enlightened by the Spirit to understand it.[3]

We read how the disciples on the road to Emmaus were positively affected when Jesus "opened their minds" and then "opened the Scriptures" to them:

> So beginning with Moses, He went through all the prophets and explained to them in all the Scriptures the things that concerned Himself... Then He opened their minds to understand the Scriptures... And they said to one another, "Didn't our hearts burn within us as He spoke to us on the road, as He opened the Scriptures to us?" (Luke 24:27, 45, 32)

---

1. I shall not mention the many ways that Psalm 119 demonstrates the power of the Scriptures to affect people. For details, see *Counsel from Psalm 119*.
2. Hebrews 4:2; 11:6.
3. According to I Corinthians 2:9–16, no one is able to appreciate and appropriate the "teachings of God's Spirit" unless he has received and possesses the Spirit.

The Scriptures Have Dunamis

The power is there to transform people, and that power is released upon regeneration and the study and application of the Word by the power of the Spirit.

The power of the Word of God is manifest from the very beginning of the Christian life. For instance, in Romans 1, verse 16, we read of the gospel as the "power of God" that leads to salvation. But the gospel is a *message*, good *news*. Such news, mixed with faith (as we have seen) leads to salvation. Faith *in the message* justifies. Also, we read that "In Him you too, by hearing the Word of truth – the good news of your salvation – when you also believed in Him, were sealed with the promised Holy Spirit." That "implanted Word," when welcomed, James says, "is able to save your souls" (James 1:21). Moreover, the Scriptures used by that Spirit give hope to the justified believer (Romans 15:4, 13). In verse 13 the Spirit is said to produce hope. In verse 4 we see that He does this not apart from but through the Scriptures. It is by the Word, which is "the Spirit's sword,"[1] that we are able to fight the battles of the Christian life successfully (Ephesians 6:17). And it must be remembered, when God sends forth His Word, it never returns to Him void, but accomplishes precisely what He intends it to accomplish (Isaiah 55:11).

In all of these passages, it is not difficult to discern something of the *dunamis* of the Word of God. Just notice the operative verbs that speak of what the Word *does*. Yet the Word does not work alone; both the Spirit and the person who is affected contribute to its effectiveness. It is the Spirit and the Word that are at work initially to transform the person; then, following regeneration, it is the Spirit and the believer who becomes a "doer of the Word" (and not a "hearer only") who together bring about growth (James 1:22).

So it is of great importance for every believer who serves Jesus Christ to recognize that the power that He needs to back up and reinforce his *exousia* comes from the Word of God,

---

1. It is said to be *His* sword because He forged and uses it as such.

which itself has *dunamis*. And as the Christian believes, appropriates, and practices, the Word adds power to his conferred authority. The importance of the written Word of power must not be minimized. When it is minimized or compromised, those who sit under weakened ministries are likely to have only "a form of godliness" while "rejecting its power" (II Timothy 3:5).

Chapter 11
Teach with Authority

The proper biblical exercise of authority in Christ's church involves several factors (which I will deal with in this chapter and chapters 12–13). The first is teaching with authority. Paul wrote to Titus, "Speak these things; urge and convict, with recognition that you have full authority to give orders. Let nobody disregard you" (Titus 3:15). That is a comprehensive command that we must unpack and apply in this and the next two chapters.

Almost every form of ministry involves teaching, whether it be preaching, counseling, guidance, instruction or whatever. In *Teaching to Observe* I note the importance of teaching in biblical counseling and I show that the Lord does not consider teaching as cramming facts into one's head, only to be regurgitated at some later time. Instead, He identifies teaching as applying His truth to people's lives so that they can better glorify Him. The command in Matthew 28:20, from which the title of the book came, reads this way: "[teach] them to observe all that I have commanded you." The passage indicates that those who are discipled to Christ must be taught to engage in commandment-oriented living rather than the feeling-oriented living that is so common today.

More than merely telling us to teach in this way, Jesus Himself became the model for all the teaching that we do. His teaching, as we have observed earlier, led people to exclaim over the difference between His teaching and the scribes' (the religious teachers of the day). How was that? We read that His listeners were "astonished at His teaching, because He taught them *as an authority*, and not as the scribes" (Mark 1:22, emphasis mine). That same fact ought to be the hallmark of the biblical teacher. Because he has an authoritative Book from God it is possible for him also to teach authoritatively. And it is incumbent upon him to do so.

Of course, no teacher today is inspired or inerrant, even with the inspired Scriptures as his guide. Teachers may misinterpret, fail to comprehend, and so on. But the teacher who knows his Bible has every reason to speak with authority when he thoroughly understands the Scriptures.

Indeed, this is a hallmark of truly biblical counseling. It ought always be said that those who counsel in God's Name give clear, straight, biblical answers (cf. Colossians 4:4). They do not hedge or provide fuzzy ideas. Now, that does not mean that every counselor has answers to every problem. But it does mean that he will honestly tell a counselee when he does not know rather than try to bluff his way through a counseling session. He will speak authoritatively only upon those matters about which he is certain.

The same is true about other teaching. I do not preach about "baptism for the dead" mentioned in I Corinthians 15:29 because I simply do not understand what Paul was referring to. I once read over thirty explanations of the passage in a journal, and every one of them convinced me until I read the next! I have always made it a policy that if I could not speak authoritatively about a matter from the Scriptures, I would not preach about that matter until I could. That is because people do not need to hear about my guesses, suppositions, suggestions, or surmises. What they need is the infallible Word of the living God presented authoritatively. Whenever someone speaks for the Lord, he should speak in a way that His Lord did and in the manner that His Word does – both of which presented truth with authority. He must not dilute that authority by some weak presentation.

Unless truth, which should be taught for the sake of life, as we saw (cf. Titus 1:1), is accurate, clear, and direct, people will not know how to live. That is one of the reasons why the church, though rich in numbers and wealth, is so poor in sturdy saints! All teachers ought to keep this in mind. It is their task to "root and ground believers in their faith" (Ephesians 3:17). That will happen when teaching itself is so solidly rooted and grounded that it can only be presented authoritatively.

Many pastors, however, came through seminaries where much speculative material was presented in theoretical, abstract form. It has been so long since they have heard truth presented authoritatively, in a form adapted to everyday living, that they do not know how to do it. Their professors so qualified every statement they made that they may have picked up that habit from them. Consequently, their congregations are served a dish every Sunday that is hard to identify as fish or fowl. Moreover, the form in which they receive it makes it indigestible. It is time that Christian teachers of every sort learn from Jesus, Who used simple language and illustrative materials, and Who told His listeners exactly what He meant in words that had the ring of certainty.

Sometimes people think it is only the hard truths that must be presented with authority. Surely, they must be – even when it is difficult for listeners to hear them. But it is also the glorious truths of our wonderful salvation that must be presented this way also. No teacher has a right to present the way of salvation in a manner that leaves his listeners with doubts. No teacher should fudge his teaching, or trim his sails, for the sake of one or two among his listeners who might be angered by what the Bible teaches. He must teach the "whole counsel of God" with all of the authority that is found in the Bible itself.

God's authoritative truth, found in His authoritative Word, must be proclaimed authoritatively by one who has been granted God's authority. How authoritative is your teaching?

Chapter 12
Exhort Authoritatively

The second fact that may be derived from Titus 3, verse 15 is that those who teach in God's Name must *exhort* authoritatively. Paul said, "Urge and convict with recognition that you have full authority to give orders." Urging and convicting have to do with applying the Word of God to the lives of the listeners to bring about the change that God requires of them. In other words, people must be *exhorted* from Scripture to hear and do what God says.

Commenting about II Timothy 4, verse 2, in which Paul urged Timothy to "reprove, rebuke, exhort," Calvin wrote, "By these words he means, that we have need of many excitements to urge us to advance in the right course." And he stresses the need for "increased vehemence and threatenings whenever necessary."[1]

This exhortation, like the teaching with which it is coupled (exhortation must grow out of teaching and may not properly be divorced from it[2]), is so authoritative that Paul insisted Titus must not allow anyone to disregard it. One may bristle under it, he may challenge it, he may get angry about it, but he must not be allowed to disregard it so that it has no effect on him – either positively or negatively.

Certainly, much of the preaching and teaching that is done today elicits very little response from listeners. Relatively few changes occur; most listeners are neither angered nor disturbed. Few are convicted of their sinful lifestyles enough to cry out for help.[3] Probably that is because, in most cases, there is so little exhortation or because that which one hears isn't authoritative. Surely there is a place in teaching for demand-

---

1. New Testament Commentary, Volume 21, p. 258.
2. Calvin also wrote, "Both exhortation and reproofs are merely aids to doctrine and, therefore, have little weight without it." Ibid.
3. See my book *How to Help People Change* for an explanation of conviction.

ing change in the Name of the Lord. Yet, sadly, in some seminaries today, preachers are taught a form of biblical-theological preaching that debases application and exhortation. Such teachers, and the preachers who follow these dictums, should reread this strong word from Paul to Titus.

The word "urge" (or "persuade") which is used here is *parakaleo*. This term is broad in scope and refers to doing whatever one finds necessary to bring about a needed result. Of course, the range of possibilities upon which one may draw is prescribed by the Bible. The word in this context clearly pertains to the use of exhortation.

A large part of successful, biblical counseling and preaching has to do with seeing that the listener not only understands, but that he also *responds* to what he is taught. A caring, effective teacher is concerned to do this *in order to change* the thinking and living of his students. That is what Paul had in mind when he told Titus not to allow anyone to "disregard" him; he was thinking of the benefit of his listeners.

People today are experts at disregarding what they hear. They let truth – God's truth – go in one ear and out the other. Many listeners have become adept at hearing in such a way that truth is stored for use with others ("Joe needs to hear this!") or for some future date when they may need to do something about the matter ("some day I may need to do this"). These are but a few of the dozens of ways people learn to disregard truth.

But good teachers do not allow this to happen. They challenge the listener to heed God's Word. In order to make a difference in the way that truth is received, any number of several possible measures may have to be taken. Principal among these is the use of strong exhortation. The matter may have to be addressed directly in an authoritative manner. Obviously, Paul (perhaps to the consternation of those who were looking over Titus' shoulder as he read Paul's letter) instructed Titus to use *full authority* and even issue *orders* to those who continued to disregard God's truth. After all, it was neither Paul's nor Titus' teaching, but rather God's, that they were avoiding. But God may not be disregarded with impunity.

It may be that the teacher is dull and uninteresting as well as unauthoritative. If these are the problems, then he must correct his manner of teaching or, if he doesn't know how to, get help. He may not misrepresent God's exciting Word by his poor, dull explanation and presentation.

And it may be that the listener hears God's truth, wants to follow it, but receives absolutely no instruction about how to put it into practice in his daily living. If the teacher knows truth only abstractly, he will not be able to help his congregation very much. He must know what it means to translate truth into day-by-day living. He must understand his listeners' difficulties and struggles. He needs to be able to offer "how-to" advice that grows out of and is consistent with the Bible at every point. The "what to" is every bit as essential as the "how to." There is no question about how Jesus taught: He accompanied the "what" with the "how."[1]

To be effective, exhortation must be given authoritatively and must not be disregarded. That is the bottom line of what Paul said. Preacher, how significant is this matter to you when you preach?

---

1. See the Sermon on the Mount, where Jesus again and again tells his listeners what to do and then explains how not to do it, followed by instructions about how to do it properly.

Chapter 13
Use Authority Fully

Paul concludes his letter to Titus by saying that he should speak and exhort "with all authority." That phrase means "with (full or complete) authority." But how far does "full authority" extend? Did those words give Titus – and elders of the church today – the right to order people around according to their own whims? The words, on the face of them, seem to grant unlimited authority. If true, that might easily turn into tyranny.

The concept of "full authority" must be understood in context. Presumably there were those who were attempting to "disregard" what Titus taught. This tendency to "think around" him (as the Greek word translated "disregard" means) had to be countered. Paul was saying that Titus should not allow this situation to continue. Rather, he had full authority to order those who failed to listen to his teaching to heed it. This order, if not obeyed, might have to be followed by the exercise of church discipline. Christian teachers may not be as frank as a teacher in Johns Hopkins University who told us, "I don't care whether you get this material or not. All I have to do is to present it!" But sometimes their presentations make you wonder. Biblical teaching involves not only imparting information, but also seeing to it that it is presented in such a way that anyone with a willing mind will "get it." Moreover, such teaching is concerned that a student will "get it" in such a practical way that he can use it. And finally, it concerns itself with whether or not the student does use it profitably in his life.[1]

In addition to those who were failing to hear Titus' sound teaching, there were also those who were rebellious (Titus

---

1. In some churches there may be concern about the disregard that many of the members show for the truth, but nothing is done to remedy the situation. Paul expected Titus to use his God-given authority directly and definitively to deal with the matter.

1:10) and some who had schismatic leanings (Titus 3:10). In the light of that situation, Paul urged Titus to use to the full the authority of Christ that had been given to him. He was not granting unlimited authority, but urging Titus not to be reluctant to use the authority that he possessed to the full. Titus was to use as much of that authority as necessary – even up to its very limit – to quell this rebellion and put down every schismatic move.

That is the problem today. Elders, to whom Christ has given adequate authority to quash divisive words and actions, fail to use that authority. Either they do not realize that they have the authority to confront and order disruptive persons to stop their nefarious activities, or, knowing this, they simply fail to do what they know they ought. Either way, because of this appalling lack of authority in many churches, people are allowed to do just about whatever they please. All to the injury of God's flock! Because of this confusion and disruption, which is due to the failure to exercise duly granted authority, many drift away from the church. They do not want to become embroiled in turmoil and controversy. But the words of Titus 1 clearly encourage the elder to exert whatever authority that is necessary to "shut the mouths" of those who are causing trouble (Titus 1:11). In how many congregations do elders do so?

It is true that one need not always use one's authority to the full. If possible, he is to "teach the trustworthy Word" in such a way that he will "encourage" listeners in living righteously (Titus 1:9). But if they reject this teaching or gainsay it, then he must "convict of their error those who object" (Titus 1:9). This "conviction" (also mentioned in Titus 2:15) consists of making out a case from the Scriptures against an offender that, were one to press it in a law court, would bring about his conviction. The word "convict" has legal implications, and was used in trying lawbreakers in court. The term has in it the idea of rebuke or reproof, but it is a rebuke that is effectively brought to bear upon an offender.

Use Authority Fully

The "rebellious persons," Paul says, were "vain talkers and deceivers." Their mouths needed to be shut by sound teaching and by the exercise of the authority of Christ because they were "upsetting whole households by teaching things that they shouldn't for the sake of shameful gain" (Titus 1:11). Obviously, these persons were becoming destructive to the infant churches that Titus was to organize on the island of Crete. And that is just the time when one must take special care to put down all attempts of such persons to "take over" and get control of these churches.

It is especially important to silence any who carry on this way at the inception of a new church because, in a small group, even one or two people can have great influence for ill. The exercise of authority, then, ought to be evident from the earliest days of a new congregation. It is, however, precisely then that elders are most hesitant to use their authority. They are looking for all the new members they can get and will often put up with the most abominable disregard for God's truth just to hold on to every person possible. That is a bad bargain! In the long run, when these persons have gained influence enough "to drag away disciples to follow them" (Acts 20:30), they will cause even greater disturbance and, in the end, the church will lose more members than if it had rejected the "vain talkers" at the beginning (Titus 3:10). Never put off dealing with divisive persons.

The exercise of authority must not be arbitrary, and it must not be used unless all teaching, exhortation, and persuasion fails. But Christ gave authority to the officers of His church to *use*. And use it they must when necessary, or they will not be good shepherds of the flock. Full use of authority in many cases would mean the use of church discipline in which, because of their contumacy, some are put out of the church. The "old leaven" is cleaned out of the church for three reasons: the honor of God's Name, the welfare of the church, and the repentance of the offender. Those who repent after exclusion from the congregation must be readmitted to their full status as members in love, forgiven by the church and given all the assistance necessary to make a good transition back into the fellowship of God's people (II Corinthians 2:6–8). For help in how to discipline in a scriptural manner, see my book *The Handbook of Church Discipline*.

Full authority also comprises a couple of other factors. It means that one may not use authority with reference to only *some* issues while avoiding others. For instance, schismatics must not be subject to discipline while gossips are not. Indeed, in some cases, gossip may lead to even more damage and division than attempted schism. Both ought to be dealt with using the full authority of which the Bible speaks. There is a tendency to avoid certain sins in the congregation while coming down too hard on others. Full use of authority, on the contrary, means to avoid none and to treat all according to the way in which the Bible directs.

Using authority to its full extent would also include exercising authority with respect to *all* persons alike. There must be no fear or favor given. Rich persons as well as poor must be treated alike. Not only ought younger men and women be urged to subject themselves to the leadership of the church, but older ones as well (Titus 2:1–8). There is a tendency to allow certain factors to influence elders in ways that are not appropriate. James speaks strongly against favoritism (James 2:1–7). To those who fall prey to this vice, he directs this question: "Haven't you discriminated among yourselves and become judges with evil thoughts?" (James 2:4). Here, James is getting at the motives involved. He asks the perpetrator to examine himself to see whether or not he is acting out of evil motives.[1] It is not our task to make judgments that distinguish who we will use discipline on and who we will not on any basis other than that which the Bible sets forth: contumacy (the unwillingness to submit to the properly exercised authority of Christ).

---

1. Notice, James does not judge another's heart, but calls upon the one whose behavior may indicate "evil thoughts" to look into his heart himself. Many today speak and write unbiblically as if they were able to know what is in another's heart.

Use Authority Fully

In all of this, the elder must avoid a tendency to be rough, harsh, and demanding. Authority must always be shown as a loving, helpful thing. Paul put it this way:

> Remind them...to insult nobody, not to be quarrelsome; to be gentle, demonstrating full consideration for every person. At one time we too were foolish, disobedient, deceived, and enslaved to various desires and pleasures, going along through life with malice and envy, hated by others and hating them (Titus 3:1-3).

What a check to the possible abuse of authority! In order not to fall into the trap of a harsh, unfeeling use of this important tool for maintaining order in the church, Paul asks those in authority to remember their own past. Before the grace of God was showered upon us in "deep affection" as it was "poured out effusively through Jesus Christ" (Titus 3:4, 6) all of us went our own willful ways. And it was only by this tender mercy shown to us by God in His Son that we were "justified by His grace" and became "heirs to the hope of eternal life" (Titus 3:7). Remembering this, in the full exercise of authority, we should "give orders" that are but a reiteration of the commandments of Christ (Matthew 28:20) in such a way that, as we deal with people, we give them no reason to reject God's good Word because of our misuse and abuse of authority. Rather, "in every way" we are to "make the teaching of God our Savior inviting" (Titus 2:10).

I have spent a good bit of time setting forth information about authority from the book of Titus. That is because this book deals with the matter so fully. Since there is no opportunity in this volume to look into every aspect of the use of authority in Titus, I encourage you to read through the book, keeping in mind that Paul is very concerned with the proper use of authority. Learn and apply what you read.

Chapter 14
Be Bold

One of the major reasons for the authority drain is fear. Elders, and many of their people, are simply afraid of what the exercise of authority may do. They fear losing members, retaliation, what others might say or think of them, and so on. Some, more wisely, fear that they may do something wrong.

The word "boldness" (*parrasia*) is a key word in the book of Acts. From the beginning to the end it appears again and again as a characteristic of the apostles who preached the the gospel from Jerusalem to Rome. What does this word mean? There are two words for "boldness" in the New Testament Scriptures. The first means "daring activity." That is not the term that we are considering. *Parresia*, the second word, means "speaking, unencumbered by fear of consequences." This sort of boldness is what every elder needs. There is nothing to fear when authority is used, as God directs, to say and do what Scripture requires. God will bless those who follow His Word and preserve them and the church that they serve.

That is not to say that there will not be trouble as the result of asserting Christ's authority. People will react. They may object. They could possibly slander. But as I said, there is nothing to fear if authority is asserted biblically. Why not? Because, I repeat, God will bless us when we follow His instructions. And authority, rightly exercised, does not *create* problems. It merely exposes already existing problems. The church needs officers who are willing to confront, to speak authoritatively, unencumbered by fear of consequences.

Remember, authority is not some passive possession of power to be used only when the elders serve the Lord's Supper. No. *Epitage*, mentioned in Titus 2:15, is a commanding, ordering authority. It is one that, if not heeded, warns about the possibility of also using the elder's binding and loosing authority. And further, when that warning is disregarded, it is an authority that proceeds to the process of church discipline.

Boldness (*parresia*) is a quality that God gives; it is not one that is native to sinners. Even the apostles prayed for boldness, saying, "So now, Lord, take note of their threats and give Your slaves all the boldness needed to speak Your Word" (Acts 4:29). And Paul, whom we rightly consider a brave man, urged the Ephesians to "pray... that I may speak boldly, as indeed I should" (Ephesians 6:19, 20). If elders want to become the right sort of elders, speaking boldly with Christ's authority, they should ask God to work boldness in them as they read the Scriptures and seek to implement what they read when authority is needed. It should help to recognize that even the apostle Paul had problems with exerting authority and had to ask churches to pray that he would be bold enough to do so. If he needed to ask, so do you.

Boldness is not crudeness. Nor is it brashness. It is certainly not the assertion of one's own opinions or insisting on his own way. It is a matter of bringing the truth of God's Word to bear on a situation in which people are not obeying it. Always that boldness must come from a proper assurance that one has interpreted God's Word as he should. Boldness will always diminish in proportion to one's uncertainty about his correct interpretation of a text. A preacher or ruling elder must be able to say, "Thus says the Lord," with a confidence that is born out of careful exegesis. So another reason for lack of boldness in asserting authority is uncertainty. Doubtless, many refuse to speak with authority because they are not sure enough about what they have to say. They are correct in not speaking authoritatively under those circumstances. But they are not right in allowing the situation to persist. If they do not understand the Scriptures adequately enough to make definite statements about matters of discipline and so on, they should take the time and make the effort to learn the answers that they need. There is no excuse for elders either not knowing what to do as elders or not caring enough to find out.

If you are not as bold in what you do and say as an elder, what is your problem? Is it fear? Is it lack of concern? Is it failure to discover the answers to questions due to lack of effort on your part? What is it? Whatever the problem, it is your obligation to pinpoint it and remedy it. Ask God to help you learn what it is – and to help you to become bold!

Chapter 15
The Other Side of the Equation – Submission

I would be remiss to speak of authority and not discuss the relationship of those who are under that authority. Authority means nothing if there are not individuals over whom one has authority, those who acknowledge that authority and submit to it. In such a relationship, there is one who *yields* and one who *wields* authority. Accordingly, when the Bible speaks of authority, it also implies *submission*.

Paul introduces the matter of authority and submission in this way: "Submit yourselves to one another out of respect for Christ" (Ephesians 5:21). He proceeds in chapters five and six to discuss three applications: the submission of wives to their own husbands, the submission of children to their parents, and the submission of slaves to their masters. In each of these relationships, what Paul has in view is the way in which *Christian* wives, children, and slaves are to submit to one in authority.[1]

But what does "submission" mean? What does it require of the one who is to submit? The word *upotasso* is a military term that means to subordinate oneself to another of higher rank. In the Scriptures, it has to do with the role one has in a given context in relationship to other persons. It has nothing directly to do with *dunamis*. One may have much greater inner authority (*dunamis*) than another, while at the same time standing in a lesser *exousia* relationship to him. The person with the uniform may not possess as much *dunamis* as

---

1. Some, quite erroneously, take verse 21 to say that all Christians, regardless of their role and their authority, must submit to one another. If correct, that understanding of the verse would, of course, destroy the authority/submissions relationships Paul was about to discuss. No one would have authority over another since everyone would be required to submit to everyone else. Even a little thought should convince those who are anxious to break down the authority of husbands over wives that this rather silly attempt is futile.

59

the one over whom he exercises *exousia*. While that is not the ideal situation in the church, in a world where all is not perfect, one may often encounter it. Submission, as we are dealing with it in this chapter, then, has largely to do with *exousia*.

To submit oneself to an officer of the church means to recognize that God has granted authority to the church, and that authority must be obeyed. It is not another person's *dunamis* to which he submits, but to his God-given *exousia*. Therefore, we are dealing specifically with elders, who are appointed to the only office that carries church authority. They are ordained (set apart, appointed) to the work of "managing" (*proistemi*) the body of people gathered together to constitute a church in a given area. Paul wrote:

> Now we ask you, brothers, to recognize those who labor among you, and *manage* you in the Lord, and counsel you. Think quite highly of them in love because of their work. Be at peace among yourselves (I Thessalonians 5:12, 13; emphasis mine).

This "managing" task is the primary concern for elders. In writing to Timothy, Paul spoke of "the elders who *manage* well" receiving "double pay."[1] He mentioned also those who, in addition to managing, also preached and taught. All elders manage as the fundamental task assigned to them, but some also carry out the two additional functions of preaching and teaching. Thus the eldership is one office, embracing two functions.

It is in the fundamental managing function that the elder's authority basically exists; here is what the writer of Hebrews had to say:

---

1. That Paul referred to double *pay*, not honor (as the King James Version wrongly translated the Greek word *time*) is plain from the Old Testament verses that are quoted in the next verse (v. 18) which speak of not muzzling the ox and paying a worker the wages he has earned. One wonders what it was that induced the translators to err when the correct translation was so obvious.

The Other Side of the Equation – Submission

Obey your leaders and submit to them. They are keeping watch over your lives as men who will have to give an account. Obey so that they may do this with joy and not as a burden, since that wouldn't be to your advantage (Hebrews 13:17).

There is no doubt, then, that the office of elder carried authority. When an elder functioned as a "manager" who "kept watch" over the flock, from time to time he would find it necessary to issue orders (not always in a formal way, of course) that should be "obeyed." Again, in this passage, the reader is told to "submit" to him because of this authority. It is this requirement of submission that turns off so many today.

There is a sinful built-in bias against authority, as I noted earlier, which causes many to bristle when someone speaks of "submitting" and "obeying." This bias is often found even in Christians. But it is a bias that they must overcome. While it is important to call upon elders to recognize and use their God-given authority according to the biblical principles that govern it, it is every bit as important to call upon members to acknowledge that their authority is from God and to submit to it!

When facing the prospect of submitting to an elder, a Christian must immediately check the feelings that may arise from his inner tendency to rebel. He should not say or think, "Who is Joe to tell me what to do or not to do?" If he does, he has a problem with submission and must deal with it. Submission does not come easily to those who from birth have had the desire to be autonomous. But a person can begin to develop a new attitude if he will only recognize that, ultimately, it is not to the elder himself that he submits, but to the Lord in Whose Name the elder speaks.

Once more, reader (especially if you are struggling with the idea of submission right now), remember that you do not ask the policeman whether he is a good husband and father before you are willing to receive a ticket from him. You remember that he functions as an arm of the state, acting under its authority. And, moreover, you remember that this authority ultimately comes from God. So to submit to the policeman – or to the elder – is to submit to God.

"I know it says so, but how come I have to submit to him? He's only another member of the church – just as I am."

Before going further, let me remind you of Korah's rebellion in which he and others were saying much the same thing. They, too, called *all* the people "holy," as if they all had the same authority. But the very word "holy" means that something is set apart from others similar to it for a special purpose. That is exactly what calling men to take upon themselves the work of the elder is all about: it is the setting apart of some qualified men for the special purposes of "managing," and "preaching and teaching." Every organization – including the church – must have leaders and must grant them authority to lead.

"Well, yes. I know intellectually that this must be so. The verses that you have cited unmistakably teach what you are saying, but there is still something that doesn't seem right about 'submitting' to someone who lives down the street from me!"

If the policeman we've used as an example lived down the street, would you still need to submit to him if he were to give you a ticket?

"Yeah. I guess so. But if I knew him well, as a friend, then it would be easier. I know that if he had to do so but didn't want to since he was a friend, I could take it better."

Ah! I think I have found one of the difficulties that you are facing. You don't look on your elders as friends. I am not sure what the reason for this is, but from your side of the relationship, at least, it is your obligation to become friendly with them. Remember the passage in I Thessalonians 5:12–13? There it says "recognize" your elders. That word, literally, is "know" them. It is your task to get to know your elders. And when you do, you must look for those things that, as Paul urges, will make you "think quite highly of them." You see, if you maintain a stand-offish attitude, you may only see them

The Other Side of the Equation – Submission

as "authoritarian" rather than as those who properly exercise authority in God's Name for your benefit.

"Okay. That helps a bit. But shouldn't they act in a friendly manner to me as well? Is this all a one-way street?"

Of course they should. In John 10, Jesus sets forth the relationship of sheep to a good shepherd. What He mentions there is that the sheep know the shepherd and his voice. And He also says that a good shepherd loves the sheep and knows each by name. In other words, there is such a close bond between them that you could describe it as nothing less than a close friendship.

"Well, I think that if I had that sort of relationship with the elders in my church, it would make a difference. You are probably right."

Certainly. I believe it would. Now, when an elder helps out a member of the flock in time of need, that goes a long way toward cementing a warm bond between them. Perhaps one of the problems is that elders do not function in the pastoral role that is everywhere designated as a primary duty of elders (cf. Acts 20, I Peter 5).

"Now you may have put your finger on it. If I saw more of my elders in a personal way, ministering to me and to other members of the flock – and even just getting to know them as friends – that surely would make a difference."

Good. Why not call upon your elder when you need help? That might be a beginning toward developing the warm relationship that you read about in John 10. And, in addition, why not invite him and his wife to dinner?

So you begin to see, don't you, that your struggle with submission may stem at least in part from your failure to make friends with your elders, and from your failing to call upon them in time of need. Turning that around, by beginning to remedy this lack, should begin to quell the struggle. Too many Christians allow their remaining sinful bias against authority to grow and dominate their view of the elder. Under those conditions, he doesn't stand a chance of helping as he was intended to.

Granted, many elders need to become better acquainted with the members of the flock. From their side of the relationship, that too needs improvement. And rather than merely attend meetings and debate and vote, elders need to be out among the members of the flock lending help to needy sheep. And they must get to know them individually. When they do, they will be of greater benefit to them and their members will be more inclined to submit whenever necessary.

Submission involves two things: *obedience*, when called for on biblical grounds, and *respect* (the word used in Ephesians 5:21). When one respects Christ's authority, he also respects Jesus Christ Himself. The word "respect" in the original is "fear." While it largely has the idea of respect, respect itself never completely loses the notion of fear.[1] To "obey you leaders" is simply to do as they say – whenever they require you to do something clearly biblical.

"What if they don't? What if they ask me to do something that is out of accord with the Bible?"

The apostles themselves settled this matter when dealing with the problem of orders that conflicted with biblical imperatives. They said "We must obey God rather than men" (Acts 5:29). Since God never gave anyone authority to command another to disobey His Word, any such command issues from "men" and not from "God." But while out of conscience toward God a person must refuse to obey any order that conflicts with Scripture, he must disagree in a respectful manner, citing the pertinent scripture passages that lead to his refusal, and explaining his interpretation of them.

So submission to elders of the church is certainly needed. And so far as possible, both elders and members must create the conditions under which submission will come easily.

---

1. The same is true of the English word "respect." If you were to ask a zoo keeper about our 500-pound gorilla, he would be likely to say, "I *respect* him; I'd be a fool to take him for granted." The note of "fear" lingers behind that use of the word respect.

Chapter 16
Limits to the Church's Authority[1]

There is no question that church authority is limited. God did not, for instance, give the church the authority to send people to jail, to put others to death, or to fight wars. Jesus made this perfectly clear when he told Pilate that His kingdom is:

...not from this world. If My kingdom were from this world, My servants would have fought to keep Me from being delivered to the Jews. But the fact is, My kingdom isn't from here (John 18:36).

It is plain, then, that the authority of the church, though very powerful, does not extend into the governmental arena. It is its own spiritual kingdom, with its own government. "It is not from here," Jesus explained. The church was not organized from among men or by them as a product of this world. Rather, it was founded by God Himself, and because its source is heavenly, the church is appropriately called "the Kingdom of God" and "the Kingdom of Heaven." These two titles refer to the very same entity, as many have clearly shown, and designate both the *Person* from Whom the kingdom comes and the *place* from which it comes. Neither the place nor the Person are earthly. So in contrasting the two governments, we see the error of wanting to extend the church's authority to earthly governments.

Neither does the church have authority to tell people how to conduct business, or any authority to choose and command individuals to marry one another. There are, however, aspects of business and of the home about which the Bible does speak. Elders do have the obligation to forbid their members to cheat others in a business transaction, and to discipline them if they do not listen. They do have authority to tell anyone that they

---

1. Here we are talking about limits to the *church's* authority, not to the authority of Christ Who has *all* authority in the heavens and in the earth (Matthew 28:18–20).

65

should not marry unbelievers, and, again, they may discipline them if they do. Indeed, if Christians are involved in governmental activities, they must follow Christian principles and practices in those areas, or they should be disciplined for not doing so.[1] In other words, although the church is not to be engaged in business, in running its members' homes, and the like, it does reach into those areas to make sure that broad-ranging biblical principles are faithfully followed.

So as long as a church member lives and acts properly within the area of these biblical principles, in whatever area of life he moves, he is under the watchful care of the elders of the flock. All such activity is subject to the scrutiny, biblical direction, and discipline of the church. But apart from becoming involved in such matters and their management of the daily affairs of the church itself, the elders have no authoritative jurisdiction over their members.

The limitation of church authority, then, extends to the business of the Kingdom of God as that is revealed in the Bible. Elders have no business dictating to members how or what they should do with reference to what cars they buy, how to grow flowers, or a hundred other matters for which there is no biblical direction. But as a Christian participates in any given activity conducted in some area other than within the government of the church itself, his action is subject to the authority and review by the church with respect to his attitudes, his words, and his behavior. These must all accord with the two great commandments: to love God with all one's heart, mind, and strength, and to love one's neighbor as oneself. In other words, if someone plants a tree too close to his neighbor's boundary line, knowing that his neighbor would be displeased, and the neighbor failed to elicit a remedy by persuasion, he would be perfectly justified in pressing charges against him in his congregation, and the offender would be subject to discipline. If in a business deal one Christian claims

---

1. Bill Clinton should have been disciplined by his church for his sinful activities, but the church had no right to tell him how to conduct his normal governmental work.

Limits to the Church's Authority

that another has cheated him, he too may bring charges against the one who allegedly did the wrong.

When discipline is rendered in favor of the complainant, and the offender acts contumaciously (unwilling to repent), he may be punished with no greater punishment than banishment from the visible church (though that is quite serious). The church has no right to have him locked up or fined as the church did in the Old Testament. The state must take care of those matters.

The fundamental difference between the theocracy in Israel and the church in this era is that there *was* a "worldly" side to the former administration, which is no longer true during this administration of the kingdom. In one sense, it was from this world. In the old order, which was done away with, the church and the state were intertwined so that actions taken by the church were also actions of the earthly government, and vice versa. The impact that this overall limitation of authority has upon the church is of great importance. Whenever the church and the state have become closely allied, both the church and the state have suffered.

The implications of the limitation of church authority reach to many of the movements that well-meaning but ill-informed Christians currently waste much energy, time, and money promoting. Instead, they ought to busy themselves and spend their money spreading the message of good news, shoring up themselves and other believers in their faith, and furthering those activities that have positive spiritual consequences – just as the apostles and the elders of the early church did.

I know this sounds like a retreatist mentality. It has been widely criticized by some in the church today. But it is not really so. It is the way in which the church has always properly furthered its influence for Christ in this world. Indeed, one sees Jesus gathering no group of people to support any cause other than the building of His church (Matthew 16:18). We see the apostles preaching the gospel everywhere, founding churches, and doing all that they can to regulate them and build up their members in their faith. We see them deeply concerned about the spiritual welfare of the saints and – so far as it involved the household of faith – the physical and monetary well-being of those who were suffering under persecution. But we do not see them building soup kitchens for the community or mobilizing forces to fight abortion and infanticide (both of which were legal evils in the Romans empire). The concern was always the soul of the individual and his eternal welfare.

As I said, this approach is often called retreatist: fleeing from the world. Wrong. Did Paul flee when he traversed the Mediterranean proclaiming Christ? Certainly not. He attacked and penetrated Satan's territory and took captives for Christ. The issue is not whether to go into the world and deal with unbelievers; it is about how one does so. It is about what he does when coming into contact with them. Is he to be involved in promoting those activities of the so-called "social gospel" (which is not the gospel at all), or is he to busy himself with spreading the good news of the Kingdom to the salvation of men, women, and children everywhere? That is the main issue.

Cities and nations have been changed for good by the latter (supposedly retreatist) approach to the unbelieving world; the former has shown no such effect upon society. Why is that? Because man's heart is the problem behind all the ills in society. You can change his outward conditions, you can change his outer behavior, but if there is no change wrought in his heart by the Holy Spirit, no lasting and truly beneficial change takes place.

That surely is one reason why the limitation of authority given to the church draws a circle around her arena of spiritual warfare (cf. II Corinthians 10) in this world and refuses to give her authority to participate in that which is outside of that circle. This circle, which hems her in, when carefully observed by the church, keeps her on the track. She has enough to keep her busy in ways that are legitimate. She does not need to take on tasks that are outside the realm of her legitimate authority, tasks to which her Lord never called her. Limits, then, are of significance to every Christian.

Chapter 17
Women in Authority?

In this age it is chic to be Politically Correct, a pitfall the church has also fallen into. Feminism, in particular, has reared her head: women want to hold positions of authority in the church. The current feminist assault on the duly constituted office of elder is a fundamental attack on Christ's rightful authority over His church. Against clear biblical instruction to the contrary, both liberals and avant guard "evangelicals"[1] claim the right to ordain women to the ministry. They have absolutely no authoritative word from the Lord allowing this. In contrast, the authoritative teaching of the Scriptures is as follows:

> Let a woman learn in silence with complete submissiveness. I don't permit a woman to teach or exercise authority over a man but to remain silent. Adam was formed first, then Eve; and Adam was not deceived, but the woman being entirely deceived fell into transgression (I Timothy 2:11–14).

In this passage, notice two things:

1. The two functions of elders are once again set forth (to teach and to rule[2]), and both tasks are closed to women.

2. The reasons given by Paul are not culturally driven, as some have claimed in order to avoid the prohibition, but are based on two of the most non-cultural events that have ever occurred: creation and the fall! Even in a perfect culture Eve was deceived.

Treating the latter reason first, it should be enough to observe that the only "culture" involved was God Himself and His perfect creation. Like it or not, those who use lame

---

1. A group to be carefully watched as the source of what may become the new liberalism.
2. See also I Timothy 5:17; Ephesians 4:11.

"reasons" such as cultural conditioning should be ashamed to do so. Instead, they simply ought to admit that they don't like the prohibition and that they refuse to submit (as Paul says they should) to it as Gods' authoritative Word in Scripture. The liberals who agree that the Scriptures do prohibit women from assuming places of authority in the church, but say that they don't believe in the inspiration of the Bible, are more honest.

A word should be spoken about the two phrases "exercise authority over" and "be silent." The word translated "exercise authority" is *authenteo* which means "to be the master over," or even "to domineer." Those translations make it abundantly clear that for a woman to arrogate to herself some dominant role over a man can only be considered a domineering act on her part.

"Aha!" someone says, "there is no explicit reference to her exercising *exousia*, then."

Don't be too sure. The meaning of the word reaches beyond *exousia* to the place where a woman, by assuming a place of authority in the church, does *more* than exercise authority over him; she arrogantly assumes a wrongful, domineering place by ruling over and authoritatively teaching the man. Instead of being in submission to his rule and teaching, she has taken it upon herself to steal and then step into his shoes! (He may not have been in his shoes to begin with in which case both are sinning.) If anything, the expression is much stronger than if Paul had merely said "exercises authority." Perhaps it should be translated "assumes a domineering position over the man."

Secondly, she is to be "in silence." She is to be "quiet." That is to say, she is not to teach or preach. Rather, she is to listen. That does not make her a cipher, as some think. We are simply talking about the role that she plays in the structure of the church. After all, it is Christ's church, and He has every right as its King and Head to structure it as He pleases. It just so happens that He decided to do things His way, for His purposes. Who are the "neo-evangelicals" to tell Him otherwise?

Women in Authority?

What cannot be tolerated is for women to rule over *men*. In Christ's order of things, that is out of order. And nothing allows a woman to bear authority over the man like granting her the eldership. Elders, as we have seen, are to be "obeyed" (Hebrews 13:17); they "manage" (literally "preside over") Christ's church (I Thessalonians 5:12, 13), and they "authoritatively instruct" (Titus 2:15) others. It is these things that the "evangelical" feminists are after. They *want* authority over men (over God?)!

This grabbing for power has all but succeeded in the "mainline" liberal churches. This is because, at its core, liberal theology is an attack upon divine authority. It fits their agenda. By seeking to undermine the Bible, they think that they may do away with its authority over them. Feminism seeking church authority blends easily with the spirit of the times and, in general, is but the latest manifestation of the liberals rejection of the Bible.

The two functions of the elder are to teach and to rule. If a person rejects the authority of Christ in the Scriptures – which Christ said "cannot be broken" – it is a simple matter to reject Paul's words to Timothy by brushing them off with "that's just an old bachelor speaking!" or words to that effect. But for those who claim to accept the Bible as their Standard of faith and practice, to reject apostolic authority is to reject God's Word, and thereby to give a lie to their stated belief in inerrant inspiration. They can't have it both ways. So they make up weak, flawed reasons for finding that the passage teaches something other than what it teaches. Actually, every one of those that is offered fails because of the reasons that Paul gives for his statements in verses 13 and 14. Those reasons – the creation order and the fall in which Eve was deceived – make no sense unless Paul was teaching that, because of these two reasons, women are forbidden authoritative leadership that involves teaching and ruling.

"Okay, I can see that what you have said is true enough concerning elders, but I understand that you think women may become deacons. Isn't that a concession on your part that makes you every bit as guilty of bucking biblical authority as the liberals and the avant guard evangelicals?"

No, it is not. One is a matter of the rejection of scriptural authority and the other is a matter of the rejection of faulty exegesis.

"What do you mean by that?"

There are those of us who believe that it is the Bible that opens the office of deacon to women, whereas that same Bible closes the office of elder to them. That is a great difference.

"That clinches it! You *do* believe in women in office!"

I am glad that you brought up the widely used phrase, "women in office," as you did because it is one that has confused many. Those who forbid women a place in the diaconate often wave it about triumphantly as a clear indication that women may not be deacons.

"Well, why shouldn't they? If women are allowed to hold a church office, that undercuts all that Paul wrote in I Timothy 2 about authority, doesn't it?"

No, it doesn't. To argue that way is to assume that those in office – *all* offices – have authority over men. But that just isn't so. The phrase "women in office" originated among people from the Christian Reformed Church where, in the consistory, both elders and deacons meet jointly, the latter in a capacity similar to "junior elders." This situation lends some semblance of truth to the argument that deacons hold an authoritative office – but that is a serious error. And to think of the diaconate as a training ground for elders compounds it! Those who think that way have a very faulty concept of the diaconate.

Office, *per se*, does not carry authority as many seem to think. That is the false premise behind your reasoning. The word "office" simply means "work," and refers to the work to which one is appointed– whatever that may be. When anyone is "ordained" (set apart[1]) to an office, that means that he or

---

1. Ordination is merely an appointment. There is nothing magical about it. Nothing is conferred but the obligations pertaining to the task. Ordination does not confer authority unless the task itself demands it.

Women in Authority?

she is appointed to a task. The office (work) of an elder involves ruling the church and officially teaching the Scriptures to its members. But the work of the deacon is quite different.

What do deacons do? First, let it be said at the outset: *deacons do not exercise authority*. They are not appointed to a task that requires authority in order to be carried out. They do not rule, and they are not official expositors of the Word.

"Well then, what *do* they do?"

They are to be (as the word literally means) "those who wait on another to do his bidding." The work of the deacon is restricted to serving Christ and His church *by serving the elders*.

The origin of the diaconate is described in Acts 6:1–7. It was born out of necessity. What was it? That tables had to be served? No. That was but the *occasion* for the formation of the diaconate; and the diaconate filled the need. But the principle behind the formation of this body was much larger: the apostles refused to leave the work to which they were called to do another sort of work. They said, "It isn't right for us to stop preaching God's Word to serve tables" (Acts 6:2). They did not think that it was "beneath" them to take care of the widows, but they recognized that doing so would keep them from the work to which Christ called them. They could not do both. So, having formed the diaconate, they could then say, "We will continue to devote ourselves to prayer and the ministry [literally "deaconing"] of the Word."[1] So the "work" to which they were appointed was to handle a task that, if done by the elders, would have kept them from *their* appointed task (v. 2–4).

Whenever elders find themselves tempted to stray from the work of serving the Word to do some non-authoritative task, they may hand over this latter work to the deacons instead of attending to the pressing need. The diaconate, then,

---

1. Here is a play on the word "to deacon." The idea is that because the newly formed deacons were serving (deaconing) tables, they could serve (deacon) the Word. The word is used throughout the passage in the original.

is a catch-all body, the one purpose of which is *to serve the elders* so that they can get on with the tasks to which they were called and ordained.

"Well, what do you know! I never thought of it that way." Many have not and, as a result, have only confused matters for themselves and for others. You see, all offices are not alike. Some involve work that requires authority to discharge. A person appointed to an office, simply put, is appointed to a particular work. To bring both offices – elder and deacon – together as if they required the same sort of work is to vitiate the very reason for the establishment of the diaconate. And to claim that both are offices requiring *exousia* is an egregious error.

"Okay. I'm tracking with you now. You may be right. But how do women fit into this office of deacon? You said that it was a matter of exegesis and interpretation, didn't you?"

Right! The debate is an exegetical one. It has nothing to do with Political Correctness. It did not originate with the feminists; though, granted, they have used it to further their cause. The issue goes back as far as the Reformation. Calvin and others advocated the position that women may be deacons. The feminists want to use the diaconate as a wedge for moving next into the eldership. And those who hold that the diaconate is an authoritative task similar to that of an elder only give them ammunition that they think fits their guns. In the Christian Reformed Church, where the idea of "women in office" is current, that is precisely what has happened. But, biblically speaking, the diaconate is a totally non-authoritative office. It is an office calling merely for service.

"I can see that but, exegetically, how can you say that women should be eligible for service in the diaconate?"

Many become bogged down discussing I Timothy 3:8–13. While a faithful interpretation of the passage leads to the conclusion that women may be deacons, the issue does not stand or fall with what I Timothy 3 says. Also take a look at Romans 16:1–2, where Paul opens the chapter with these words:

Women in Authority?

Now I want to introduce to you Phoebe, our sister, who is a deaconess [literally, "deacon"] from the church of Cenchrea, so that you may receive her in the Lord in a way that is fitting for saints, and help her in any matter in which she may need your assistance, since she, indeed, has been a benefactor of many, including me.

There are a number of things that may be pointed out from an analysis of these two verses. Presumably, Phoebe faithfully carried the letter from Paul to Rome. It might be possible to translate the word *diakonos* as "female servant," but since she is designated "a sister" it is unlikely that Paul would have repeated himself in that way. No, she was a deacon in the church of Cenchrea. She is to be welcomed as a deacon.[1]

Here, we see her about to carry out some task that had been assigned to her by the elders of her church. We have no idea what this was. Paul knew her well and had benefited from her help in the past. He now explains that she may need the help of the Christians in Rome to carry out the work that she was sent by her church to do. Once more we see the service of the deacon, here assisting others. Moreover, Phoebe is introduced in a different manner from the other women mentioned in the chapter, placing her in a different category. And, of course, she is mentioned first in the list of those to be commended. And finally, notice that Phoebe doesn't come to the church at Rome asserting her authority as a deaconess (she had none). She is *"from the church* at Cenchrea." That is to say, she was sent by the authority of the elders there. And to boot, she needs the recommendation of an apostle. There is nothing authoritative about her as a deacon whatsoever! Everything indicates that Phoebe was just what Paul says, "a deacon from the church of Cenchrea" who was on some assignment from the church to which she belonged. There is no reason to believe otherwise, and every reason to believe she bore the title of the office to which she belonged.

---

1. The feminine, *diakonissa*, is used only in ecclesiastical Greek.

In his commentary on this passage, Calvin does not hesitate to call Phoebe an *"assistant* of the Cenchrean church" and says that Paul "commends her on account of her *office."* And he also references I Timothy 5:9 as a further indication of the sort of "service" (*diakonia*) in which Phoebe had been involved in her office. Whether we can agree with the way that Calvin reconstructed Phoebe's "office" is unimportant. The crucial point is that, in Reformation times, there was no hesitancy on his part to believe that Phoebe was a deacon and had been called to an office of Christ's church. So you can readily see from the brief discussion of the diaconate that there can be a fine fit between women and the non-authoritative office. Good men, since the outset of the Protestant church, have differed about whether or not women belong in it, but they have differed on exegetical grounds.

Once more, we have seen attempts on the part of women to arrogate authority to themselves. But what is significant is that through their misinterpretation of the office as one involving authority, true Bible-believing Christians, who think that they are opposing liberalism and feminism, actually lend support to those causes. Rather than lump together deacons and elders in order to exclude women from the diaconate, they should more carefully distinguish the elements involved in the work of each. Elders are set apart to the work of teaching and ruling – authoritative tasks. Deacons are ordained to serve the elders by relieving them of any work extraneous to their tasks.

Should a deacon – man or woman – act as if his or her office grants authority to give orders in a high-handed manner, he/she should be rebuked by the elders. The overriding characteristic of a faithful deacon is helpfulness. Understood scripturally, the diaconate is a very helpful office in the church, and women, who already do much diaconal work without an appointment to the office, can be a most useful part of that body. Let's not forbid them to minister to the elders, many of whom are bogged down with all sorts of things they should not have to do.

Women in Authority?

From I Timothy 2, we have clearly seen that authority is not to be given to women; it seems equally true that women may be set aside (ordained) for non-authoritative work. And, of course, such work does not collide with the prohibitions of I Timothy 2. Jesus Christ did not set up two authoritative offices which would inevitably conflict with one another. All authority lies in the eldership. Indeed, since there can be no clash of authority in a properly functioning congregation, there ought to be a fruitful working harmony between the two bodies. That is the goal; does your church approximate it?

Chapter 18
When All is Said and Done

Yes, it all comes down to this: God is the Authority, the Source of all true authority, and the Determiner of all authority issues. He alone has the right and the ability to set standards for His church; how does anyone else dare do so? Yet that is precisely the problem; all sorts of people within the church have determined that by passing laws, shaming others, setting up lists of dos and don'ts, and the like, they can dictate what is best for the church. They set themselves up as authorities. How dare they muscle their way like that? Yet with little or no compunction, they *do* dare to do so!

Consider this: how many books do you read that attempt to ferret out what *God* has to say in His Word concerning His authority over His church? Perhaps, if you are like many others, this book is the very first that you have ever read which has that goal in mind. The matter is simply of little interest in the church. And, even here, this book opens up biblical principles and practices relative to authority only to a minimal extent. Much more needs to be said.

Go to the local bookstore. What will you find? If you read anything that directly has to do with authority at all, you will be fortunate. But if you have the eyes to see, what book after book is doing is dealing indirectly with authority issues all the time – without noting the fact. Indeed, many of the authors themselves don't have even the slightest idea of that fact. Instead, without any biblical grounds,[1] you will find piles of books that will tell you what to do in the church of Christ and how to do it.

In addition to books, the ideas of men, filched from business practices and propagated in large "spiritual" conferences by "pastoral" CEOs, have spread widely around the church as a whole. Yet most of these concepts are not only inconsistent with biblical teaching, they are antithetical to it. God's

---

1. That is to say, without any authority behind what they say but themselves!

79

authority is set aside for man's. But if you were to say this, you would be labeled a fundamentalist fanatic. Or if for some remote reason someone took your concern seriously, and looked into the principles and practices that he is being taught, it is very likely that he could not discern anything wrong with them. He would know so little of the Scriptures that he could not use them to evaluate the material. Many talk about the Bible as a standard, but wouldn't know how to use it as such if you were to spell it out in children's blocks! They are virtually ignorant of wide ranges of truth and have no idea about how to extract if from holy Scripture and apply it to everyday life! Behind all of this is an abysmal lack of concern about knowing God's Word.

After all is said and done, if God *is* the Authority – as you know He is, Christian – then you and others like you must become far more able and eager to discover and put into practice God's authoritative principles, which He has established to guide the mission of His church.

That, for many, means getting far more serious about Bible study. I said *study*, not reading. Reading some daily "devotional" won't do it. Listening to religious broadcasts won't do it. Reading books based on someone's experiences won't do it. It means hours spent every week poring over the pages of Scripture with the best Bible study helps available. It means becoming aware through that study of the many flawed ways in which Christ's work is carried on. It means doing whatever is necessary to correct erroneous ways. Finally, it means putting in place those biblical principles and practices that are authorized by Christ Himself.

After reading this book, how eager are you to do whatever it takes to help your congregation conform to the ways that God has authoritatively ordained? If so, here are some things you might do:

1. Begin to pray about the problems as you come to see them through regular, serious Bible study.
2. Continue to sharpen your understanding of your church's

When All is Said and Done

problems through careful Bible study – areas where the church is operating according to unauthorized standards.

3. By continued study, try to determine exactly what God wants done to remedy the situation.

4. Think about non-disruptive ways in which you can mention to the elders of your church what you have learned, and how you think that the problems can be solved. Carping criticism is *not* helpful.

5. Continue to pray and, in a kindly, helpful way, encourage those in charge to take their authority seriously enough to do what God requires of them.

6. *Be patient*; in time God could use you to bring about the needed change.

7. Above all things, do not become divisive. Don't gather a group together to try to pressure the authorities; don't start complaining all over the church. Rather, talk to God about the matter.

8. All in all, if you follow some such plan in a church that is basically committed to the Scriptures as the inerrant and sufficient Word of God, you may expect good results. If, on the other hand, you are in a congregation that refuses even to acknowledge the Bible as its standard of faith and practice (let alone use it that way), you'd better think about moving to another congregation that is sound in the faith.

Whatever you do, always stand behind and submit to true authority. Enhance it by your life and by your words. Never do anything to denigrate it in the eyes of others. There is all too little authority in the church; when you find some, rejoice, be grateful, and ask God to multiply it! When God's authority in all things is recognized in the church, when He is given His rightful place, He blesses. Does your church need blessing from Him? Could it be that the reason it lacks blessing is because of its lack of true authority from God?